ARE YOU LONESOME
TO-NIGHT ?
Words & Music by ROY TURK & LOU HANDMAN

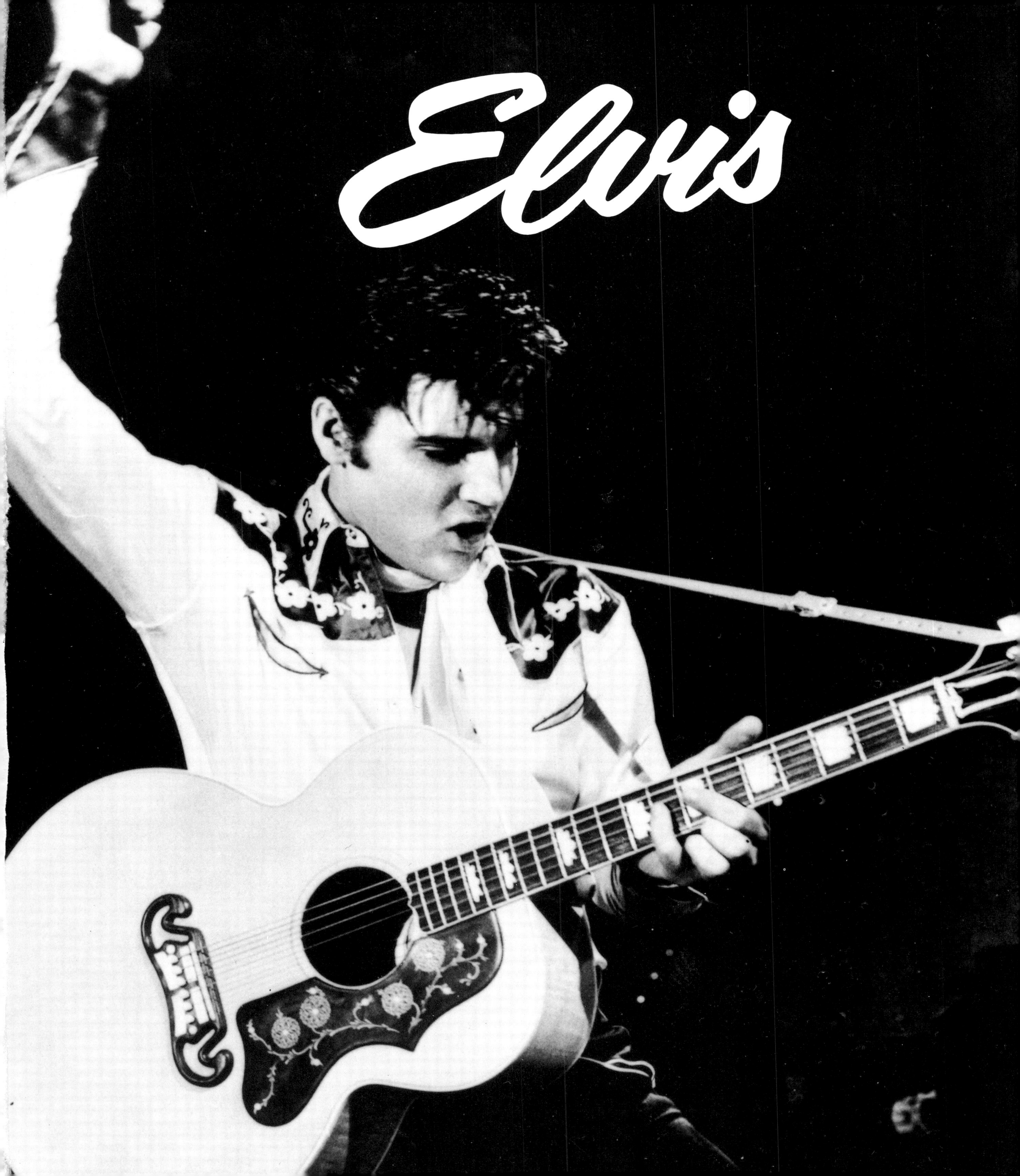
Elvis

Text
William Allen

Commissioning editor
Andrew Preston

Design
Philip Clucas

Editors
David Gibbon
Nicola Dent

Picture Research
Leora Kahn

Picture Sources
London Features International
Michael Ochs Archives/LFI
The Neal Peters Collection
FPG International
The Bettmann Archive
Photofest
CLB International
William Allen

5021
This edition published in 1997
by Colour Library Direct
© 1992 CLB International
    Godalming, Surrey
All rights reserved
ISBN 1-85833-669-4
Printed and bound in China

Elvis

Colour Library

Introduction

ELVIS PRESLEY, THE MOST successful performer in the history of popular music, died on August 16, 1977, aged forty-two. His death was followed by nationwide mourning, scenes of mass hysteria, and a flood of media coverage of the kind that had not been seen since the death of President Kennedy. Newspapers gave the event the kind of coverage normally reserved for leading statesmen, and President Jimmy Carter, in an unprecedented gesture regarding a pop star, made a public statement saying, "Elvis Presley's death deprives our country of a part of itself. His following was immense, and he was a symbol to the people the world over of the vitality, rebelliousness and good humor of this country." Similar tributes poured into Presley's home, Graceland, from all corners of the globe, most notably from fellow performers of different generations, including Bing Crosby, Frank Sinatra, Sammy Davis Jr., Elton John, and other rock singers and groups.

ON AUGUST 18, WHEN ELVIS was buried, over 150,000 fans lined the four-mile funeral route from Graceland to Forest Hills Cemetery. Many of them had flown in from as far as Japan, Australia and England. That same day, while the fans were watching the funeral procession, sales of Elvis' last album, *Moody Blue*, rocketed to 250,000 and shops the world over were selling out of every Elvis disc, book and poster in stock.

MOST OF THE AMERICAN NATION, and much of the world, was in an unprecedented state of shock.

"ELVIS PRESLEY WAS AN EXPLORER OF VAST NEW LANDSCAPES OF DREAM AND ILLUSION. HE WAS A MAN WHO REFUSED TO BE TOLD THAT THE BEST OF HIS DREAMS WOULD NOT COME TRUE, WHO REFUSED TO BE DEFINED BY ANYONE ELSE'S CONCEPTIONS."
Dave Marsh, *Elvis*

"LET IT BLEED."
Elvis Presley, on singing

Graceland, Memphis, Tennessee. Flowers for a dead King.

AFTER ELVIS' DEATH, HIS record sales soared to over one billion. The Presley shack in Tupelo, Mississippi, and his mansion, Graceland, in Memphis, Tennessee, became national shrines attracting hundreds of thousands of visitors each year, many of them flying in from overseas. Streets were named after him. Elvis imitators were soon numbered in the hundreds. More than a thousand items of "Presleyana," including jewelry, sunglasses, cups and saucers, soap, car licence plates, and even panties bearing his picture and song titles, were being sold faster than they could be produced. The Presley industry grew and grew, thus keeping him, even years after his passing, among the world's top ten show business money-spinners.

"ONE DAY THERE WON'T BE ANY MORE POP OR COUNTRY OR RHYTHM AND BLUES. IT'LL JUST BE NAMED AMERICAN MUSIC, AND ELVIS PRESLEY DID AS MUCH TO MAKE THAT AS ANYONE WHO EVER LIVED."
J.D. Sumner

Elvis has often been credited as the first white man to popularize black music. In fact, the first to do so was the plump, middle-aged Bill Haley (above), whose hit "Rock Around the Clock" created a worldwide sensation before Elvis came along. Nevertheless, it was Elvis who became a teen favorite from his earliest appearances in Tupelo, Mississippi (left) while Haley sank into relative obscurity.

SO GREAT WAS THE continuing grief over his passing that records and tapes of Elvis speaking from beyond the grave made small fortunes. Books by clairvoyants, mediums and other "after life" practitioners also earned a mint. Finally, rumors began circulating to the effect that Elvis was still alive and had merely gone into hiding to avoid his own fame. Grainy photos of an alleged "Elvis" in cars, hotels and even supermarkets were reproduced in countless newspapers worldwide. A taped message from the supposedly still living Elvis was sold with a book detailing why he had gone into hiding. By 1988 it was possible to buy an "Elvis on Tour, 1988" T-shirt, which actually listed the many places where Elvis had reportedly been spotted or photographed since his supposed death.

A two-year-old Elvis was said to have left his mother's side in church to stand with the local choir. Joining in to sing with his parents, friends and church, he rapidly grew in confidence and experienced a variety of styles.

BY 1991 EVEN A heavyweight British newspaper, the *Independent*, felt compelled to devote a full three pages to the Presley phenomenon, pointing out *en passant* that hardly a week now passes in which Johnny Carson, America's most popular chat-show host, doesn't make an "Elvis is alive" joke.

IN 1979 THE PRESLEY estate was worth approximately $1 million. By 1991 this had grown to more than $75 million and the estate, which includes Presley's Memphis mansion, Graceland, now open to the public, was making an estimated $15 million a year in gross income. In 1991 more than 670,000 fans filed through its rooms. This already remarkable figure is expected to increase dramatically in August 1992, which marks the 15th anniversary of Elvis' death.

CLEARLY, ELVIS PRESLEY WAS an extraordinary phenomenon.

THIS IS HIS STORY.

10

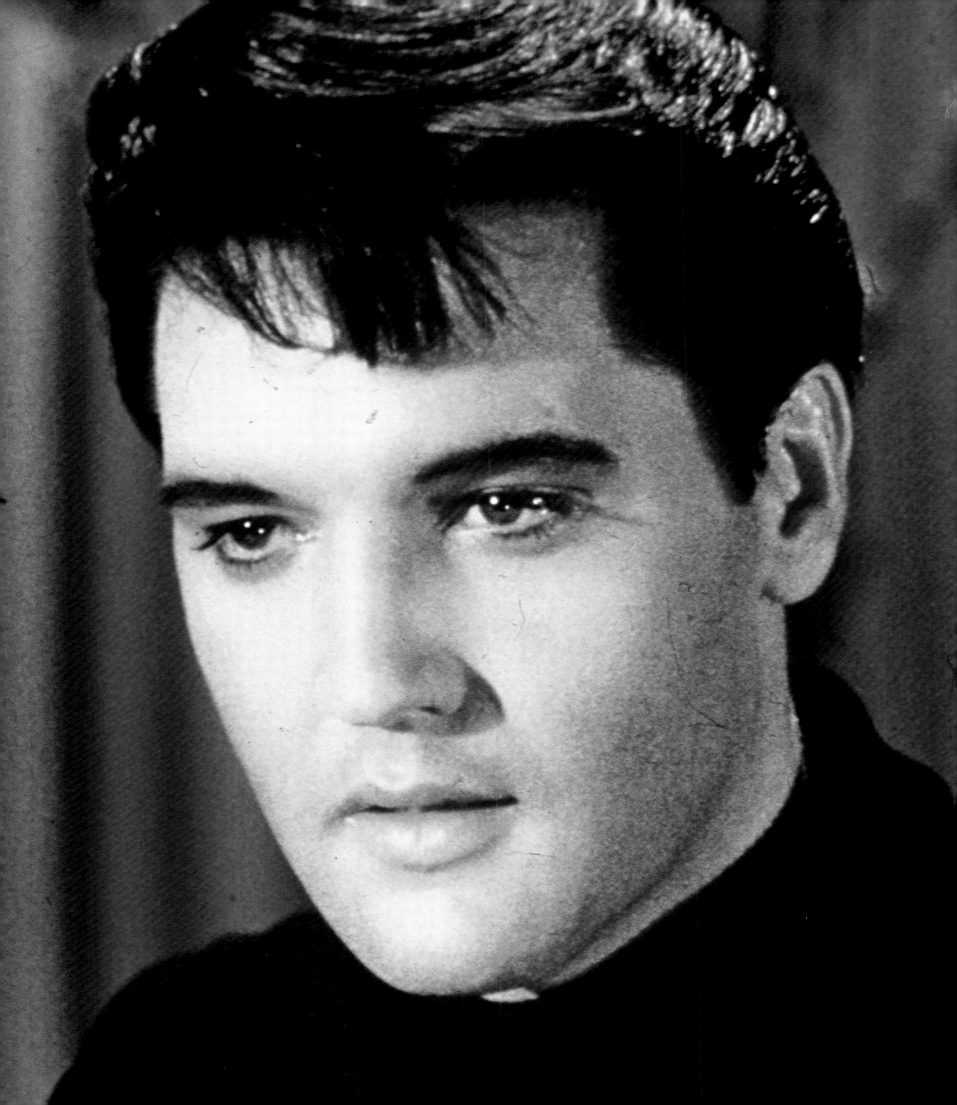

Elvis' exotic good looks, flashy clothes and wild performing style soon had the kids clamoring for his autograph.

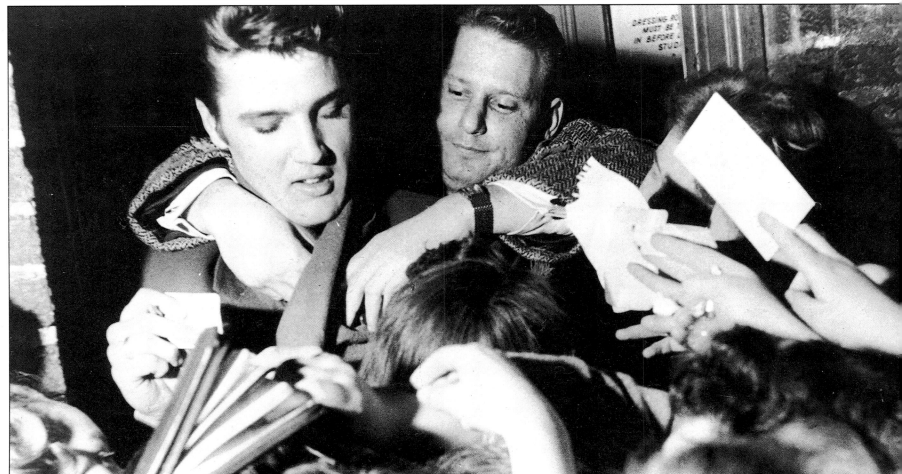

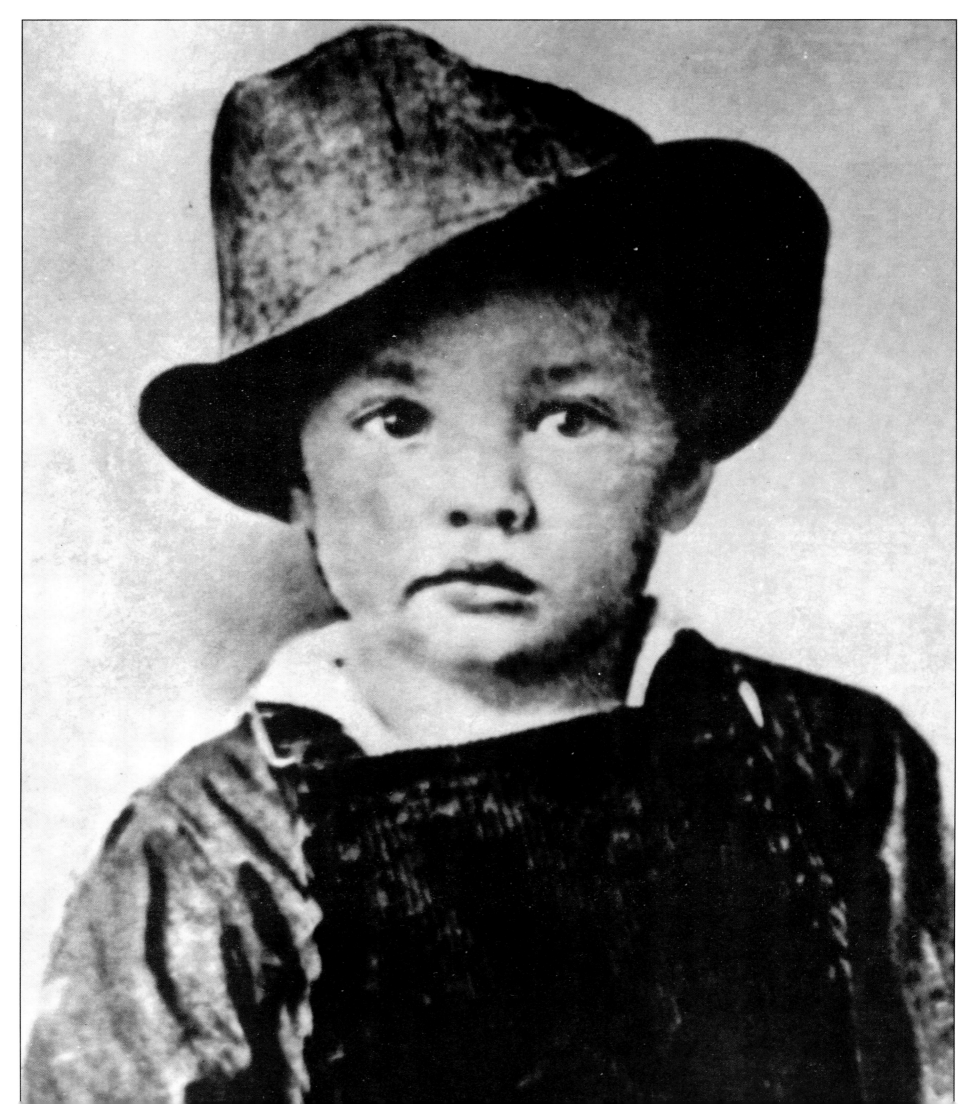

History in the Making

"Oh, I wish I was in the land of cotton,
Old folks there are not forgotten."

An American Trilogy

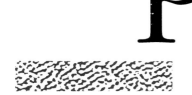

Elvis came from poor people and was born in a modest shack in Tupelo, Mississippi, built by his sharecropper father, Vernon Presley. Left: the three-year-old Elvis' distinctively curled upper lip was evident right from the start.

"EVEN – PERHAPS ESPECIALLY – IN THE SOUTH, THEY TALK ABOUT ELVIS AND JESUS IN THE SAME BREATH. THERE'S A GOOD REASON FOR THAT. ELVIS WAS THE FIRST PUBLIC FIGURE SINCE JESUS THAT COULDN'T BE IGNORED BY ANY SEGMENT OF HIS CIVILIZATION."
Greil Marcus, *Dead Elvis*

PROBABLY THE MOST MEMORABLE man in the history of American music, Elvis Presley was born in a two-room plank house in East Tupelo, Mississippi, on the wrong side of the railroad tracks. The small house, or shack, is located along the Old Saltillo Road, almost opposite the Methodist church. The people who lived in it were Vernon and Gladys Presley.

THE LINE ON ELVIS PRESLEY'S maternal side goes back at least as far as a full-blooded Cherokee Indian, Morning Dove White, buried in Hamilton, Alabama, in 1835. Morning Dove White married a white man, William Mansell, from South Carolina. The Mansells originated in Le Mans, France, but they moved to England, mixed with the Scots, went from there to Ulster, and ended up in America as Scots-Irish. William Mansell's father fought in the Revolution, and Mansell himself fought twice against the Indians with General Andrew Jackson in Alabama, Georgia and Florida. In 1818 he returned to Tennessee and married Morning Dove White.

WITH MANY OTHER SCOTS-IRISH, Mansell and his Cherokee bride joined the great migration of 1820 into the promised land of Alabama, and settled in Marion County, near the Mississippi state border. They became farmers. Morning Dove White gave birth to three children, including a daughter, Morning Dizenie, who married Russell Palmer, doctor and landowner, and gave birth to twelve children. Most prospered, and one, Dr. Alexander Sherman Palmer, was distinguished enough to be given over a page in Biddle's *Notable Men of Alabama* (1893). The Mansell's eldest son, John, half Scots-Irish, half Indian, married Elizabeth Gilmore and produced ten offspring. His sons, including White Mansell, eventually left Marion County and by 1880 were settled near the town of Saltillo, part of Lee County, Mississippi, whose county seat was Tupelo.

"TUPELO" IS A CHICKASAW INDIAN word describing either a lodging place, a

15

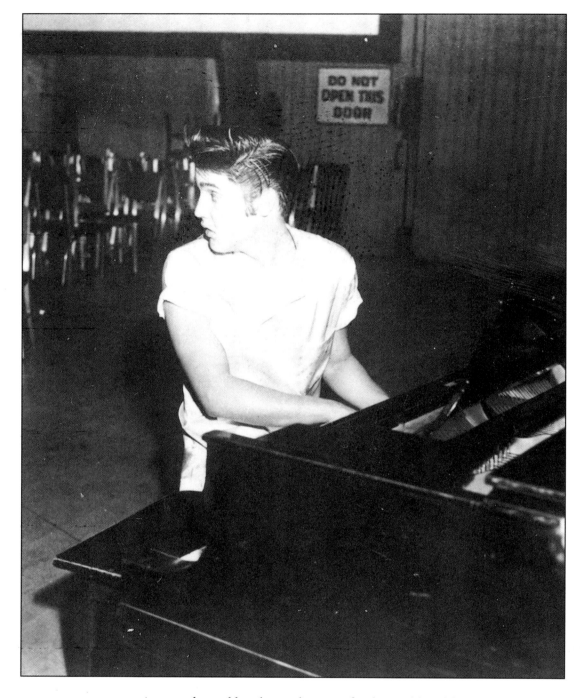

Although Elvis is widely associated with the guitar, which he played reasonably well, his favorite instrument was in fact the piano, which he learnt at an early age and played at every opportunity. Elvis had free piano lessons in Tupelo from his uncles, Johnny and Vester, the preacher Frank Smith, and local country singer, Mississippi Slim. During his final concerts he even played piano on stage.

gum tree, or a magic wand used by the Indians to find good land for settling. Many sons of Tupelo died in the Mexican War of 1846-8. The Yankees raided the town repeatedly during the Civil War, and the last battle of that war was said to have been fought there. The town is noted for cattle breeding and cotton growing.

THE THIRD MANSELL SON, White, settled in Tupelo and married Martha Tackett, who was Jewish. The marriage produced four children, including Elvis Presley's maternal grandmother, Octavia Luvenia (*Lucy*) Mansell. On September 20, 1903, Lucy married a handsome neighbor, Robert Lee Smith, who also had Indian blood in him. The marriage produced nine children and one of them, born April 25, 1912, in White Mansell's last house in Pototoc County, was Elvis Presley's mother, Gladys Love Smith.

GLADYS WAS THE LAST of four girls in a row, but two younger brothers followed, then another daughter and son. When Gladys was five, the family moved back to Lee County, traveling in an open wagon. They settled into "the sorriest shack on the Wilburn farm" in Gilvo, about four miles from Tupelo.

ROBERT LEE SMITH, A decent man, was useless at farming, but he soon gained a reputation for making good "moonshine" whisky. When not sharecropping or moonshining, he took on any work he could find, but Lucy was suffering from TB (tuberculosis), and also had expensive tastes, so the money always disappeared quickly. Being constantly ill, Lucy placed a heavy burden on her daughters. They not only had to look after the household, but also worked the fields as sharecroppers from an early age, attending school only during the winter months.

GLADYS LOVE SMITH GREW into a beautiful, dark-eyed woman whose smile hid the fears engendered by constant hardship and the ever-present possibility of her mother's death.

NEVERTHELESS, SHE COULD SING and dance. She loved the sexually suggestive songs of Jimmy Rodgers, and often sang to them. She also learned to sing in the Holiness churches she attended, charismatic fundamentalist churches, where in Gladys' younger days the hymns were based on the blues, the pastor would often have a guitar, and both preacher and congregation would be physically exuberant in the manner of Pentecostal churches. Gladys also had a notable talent for "buck" dancing, which is performed alone and requires a total abandonment to one's innermost feelings. So good was Gladys at this that one neighbor was reduced to tears each time she saw her do it. Another insisted that Elvis Presley inherited his sense of rhythm from his mother.

THOUGH GLADYS STILL HAD fears about the possibility of her mother's death from TB, it was her father, Robert Lee, who died suddenly from pneumonia. He was buried in an unmarked grave in the Spring Hill Cemetery.

WITH NO ONE TO PROVIDE for them, the family was split apart. The invalid Lucy went to live with a married daughter and her husband. Gladys' brother Travis went to work as a hired hand. The rest of the family, including Gladys, moved in with one of Granny Smith's sons in Eggville, Lee County.

IN DECEMBER, 1932, IN the middle of the Great Depression, Gladys went to work as a $2 per day sewing-machine operator at the Tupelo Garment Center. There she became friendly with girls from the east side of Tupelo, which was separated from the main town by a levee, a mile-long stretch of cotton and corn fields, and the railroad tracks. Though East Tupelo was considered to be on the wrong side of the tracks, Gladys liked it. She moved into a rented house in Kelly Street with her brothers and sisters.

WHEN SHE WAS TWENTY-ONE years old, Gladys fell in love and eloped with a handsome neighbor, Vernon Elvis Presley.

VERNON WAS BORN IN FULTON, Mississippi, in 1916, to Jessie D. McClowell

Below: Elvis with his mother – as he grew more handsome, she was rapidly ailing and visibly aged.

"I HAVE A ROOM WITH SOME ELVIS PICTURES IN IT. I HAVE A ROOM WITH LOTS OF PICTURES OF ELVIS .... YOU DON'T FIND HIM FASCINATING?"
Eddie Murphy

Presley and Minnae Mae Hood. The Presley family has been traced back to Andrew Presley, a Scots blacksmith who emigrated to North Carolina. He had three sons: Andrew Presley Jr., who fought in the Revolution, Dunnan Presley, who became a Tennessee wanderer, and, Dunnan Presley Jr., another colorful Southern character who married four times and deserted twice during the Civil War. One of his wives, Martha Jane Wesson of Fulton, Itawamba County, gave him two daughters, one of whom, Rosella, was J.D. Presley's mother. Rosella was a sharecropper and reputedly had some of her ten children by a man who was part Cherokee, which gave her something in common with Gladys.

ROSELLA'S SON, J.D. PRESLEY, was always in fierce competition with his brother, Noah. The latter, who was widely known as the "good" brother, became mayor of East Tupelo and was credited with being responsible for most of its improvements during that time. J.D., on the other hand, was the good-looking "bad" brother who drank a lot, was as "mean as hell," and made life miserable for his wife and son.

VERNON INHERITED HIS FATHER'S exceptional good looks, but his father gave him a hard time and he lived in fear of him. Perhaps for this reason Vernon grew into a handsome, charming, unambitious young man who drifted from one low-paid job to the next, including sharecropping, truck driving, and general laboring.

GLADYS AND VERNON ELOPED and were married on June 17, 1933, when she was twenty-one and he only seventeen. Vernon was then living with his parents, brother Vester, four sisters and a lodger, in a big house on the Old Saltillo Road. If good at little else, Vernon was good with his hands, and with money borrowed from local dairy farmer Orville Bean, he built the Presley shack in 1934.

GLADYS BECAME PREGNANT THE following year. What she did not know, but what we know in retrospect, is that any child born of Gladys and Vernon Presley would be a unique mixture of Cherokee, Scots-Irish, and Jew, with the dark good looks of the Mansells intermingled with the blond handsomeness of the Presleys. Such a child would also be impulsive, adventurous, generous, good-humored, God-fearing, essentially humble, and musical.

LIKE ALL PROUD MOTHERS, Gladys felt that her child would be unique. In this case, she was right.

Elvis' unique, slightly androgynous features were inherited from his part Indian ancestry, his mother's dark-eyed, delicate beauty, and his father's rugged, man-of-the-soil good looks. Combined with Elvis' famous curled lip and extraordinary voice, they would lead him from obscurity to unprecedented fame, with streets in Memphis and Tupelo renamed in his honor and a statue unveiled in the Hilton Hotel (formerly the Hotel International), Las Vegas, where he had broken all attendance records.

From Tupelo to Memphis

"I never knew a guitar-player worth a damn."

Vernon Presley

Less than twenty-one years after being born, Elvis would be causing hysterics at his rock-and-roll concerts. Typical was the reaction of this audience (left) at his charity benefit at Russwood Park, Memphis, on May 7, 1956.

"IT WAS LIKE HE CAME ALONG AND WHISPERED A DREAM IN EVERYBODY'S EAR AND THEN WE DREAMED IT."
Bruce Springsteen

ON JANUARY 8, 1935, Gladys Presley gave birth to twin boys, Jesse Garon and Elvis Aaron. Jesse Garon was stillborn. He was buried forty-eight hours later in a shoe box in an unmarked grave in the Princeville Cemetery.

MANY OF THOSE WHO knew the Presley family at this time were aware of Gladys' overwhelming love for Elvis and viewed it as a natural response to the death of his twin. Gladys was often credited with psychic intuition when it came to Elvis, and he often claimed the same about her. He also talked in later years of feeling incomplete without his stillborn twin and would often visit Jesse Garon's grave to "talk" to him. He called his missing brother his "psychic soulmate."

ON APRIL 5, 1936, approximately three months after Elvis was born, a catastrophic tornado tore through Tupelo, killing 235 people, injuring 350, and destroying forty-eight city blocks. Though the tornado razed St. Mark's Methodist church, the Presley shack directly opposite remained untouched.

GLADYS AND VERNON WOULD frequently refer to this as a miracle, and the former, in particular, took it as a sign that her surviving son was truly someone special. She instilled this conviction in Elvis right from the start, which gave him confidence despite his natural shyness.

ON NOVEMBER 16, 1937, when Elvis was three, Vernon was convicted of forging a check and sentenced to two years in the notorious Parchman Penitentiary. His good behavior and the relentless lobbying of the townsfolk of Tupelo got him out after nine months. Nevertheless, Vernon's imprisonment had a profound effect on the young Elvis, making him more dependent upon, and simultaneously protective of, his mother.

WHILE VERNON WAS SERVING his time, Gladys moved in with her first cousin, Frank Richards, where he lived with his family on Maple Street in South Tupelo.

Released from prison, Vernon joined them. There, the humiliation and hardship caused by Vernon's imprisonment led all three Presleys to suffer restless nights, with Elvis sleep-walking from then until well into his teens.

FROM AN EARLY AGE Elvis found escape from reality by reading comics, including *Superman*, *Batman*, the *Plastic Man* and, particularly, *Captain Marvel*.

ELVIS TOOK HIS HAIR color and style (sideburns and forelock) directly from drawings of Captain Marvel. Years later, when he was famous, the Presley capes and lightning-bolt emblem on the TCB (Taking Care of Business) and TLC (Tender Loving Care) jewelry, as well as the lightning bolt on the tail wing of his airplane, the *Lisa Marie*, were also taken from *Captain Marvel*. Indeed, Elaine Dundy (*Elvis and Gladys*) argues persuasively that Elvis' whole personality – the humility, humor, and desire to save the world and his family – was based on this popular comic book character.

IN 1940, THE PRESLEYS moved for a six-month period to Pascagoula, near Biloxi on the Gulf of Mexico, where Vernon worked in the shipyards. Back in Tupelo, the family shared a house on Reese Street.

VERNON MANAGED TO STRUGGLE along on various public projects, including the building of public lavatories, but in 1942, when the United States entered the Second World War, he left home again to help build a prisoner-of-war camp in Como, Mississippi, 173 miles from Tupelo. In his absence, Gladys, pregnant again, had a miscarriage and was taken into the Tupelo Hospital. The seven-year-old Elvis walked alongside the stretcher, holding her hand and crying.

THE LOSS OF ANOTHER child made Gladys even more obsessively protective of Elvis.

VERNON'S JOB IN COMO finished in May 1943, but he found more industrial work in Memphis. During his long absences, the bond between Elvis and Gladys became virtually unbreakable, with Elvis more determined than ever to look after his mother in the future.

IN 1945, WHEN THE war ended, Vernon returned to Tupelo and put a deposit on a brand new, four-room house on Berry Street. Eleven months later, unable to keep up the mortgage payments, he was forced to sell and move his family into an old shack on Mulberry Alley, located over the highway, near the city dump. From there, they moved to 1010 North Green Street (now Elvis Presley Circle), on the edge of Shakerag, Tupelo's "black" section.

GLADYS AND ELVIS MUST have assumed that things couldn't get worse, but in September 1948 bad luck struck again when Vernon, working as a truck-driver, was dismissed. In late September or early October of 1948, he and Gladys packed the family belongings in boxes, loaded them onto a 1939 Plymouth, and headed for Memphis, Tennessee, where Elvis, already a singer, would become a sensation.

ELVIS SANG FROM AN early age. Vernon and Gladys attended the First Assembly of God church on Adam Street, Tupelo, and there, when Elvis was only

"I THOUGHT HE WAS A BLACK GUY WHEN I HEARD HIS SUN RECORDS... EVERYBODY KNEW HE WAS GOING TO BE THE HOTTEST THING IN SHOW BUSINESS."
Chet Atkins

22

two years old, he impulsively left his mother's side to scramble up on the stage and join in with the choir. He also sang with his parents at church and social functions, or simply for friends, which they were called upon to do often.

GOSPEL WAS ALL PERVASIVE. One of Elvis' favorite gospel singers and boyhood idols was Jake Hess, leader of the Statesmen Quartet, who recorded "How Great Thou Art" long before Elvis made it a staple of his 1970s concerts. Elvis also heard gospel on the radio, listening regularly to the broadcasts of Sister Rosetta Tharpe and numerous gospel groups. Later he would claim to know practically every religious song ever written.

"IT MORE OR LESS puts your mind to rest," he said in the documentary movie, *Elvis on Tour* (1972). "At least it does mine – since I was two." He also got some of his uninhibited body movements from the black and white preachers of his early days. "They cut up all over the place, jumpin' on the piano, movin' ever' which way. The audience liked them. I guess I learned from them."

HE WAS ENROLED IN East Tupelo Consolidated school in 1941, when he was six years old. While the school was on the wrong side of the tracks, it was well disciplined and had a good educational record. That Elvis was an average student may be due to the fact that already he was obsessed with the notion of becoming a singer.

ELVIS HAS BEEN REPORTED widely as an over-protected child, but he was clearly out of Gladys' sight a lot. At the tender age of eight he was hitching rides every week to the "Saturday Jamboree" country music program of the local radio station, WELO, located on Spring Street, Tupelo. There, according to former "Jamboree" announcer Charlie Boren, Elvis regularly got up to sing everything from gospel to country, even World War II songs. However, his favorite was Red Foley's classic weeper, "Old Shep," about the love of a boy for the dog that saves his life, then has to be put down. Elvis also developed a strong case of hero worship for one performer in particular: the country singer and guitar-plucker, Mississippi Slim.

AMONG THE MANY WHO gave Elvis lifts to town was part-time musician Reggie Bell, who played with the Lee County Ramblers. Bell often took Elvis to the WELO studios when he was playing and let him sit there listening, either to the Ramblers or to Mississippi Slim. Eventually, Elvis charmed his way into Slim's favors. Slim was no great performer, but he could wail a good country weepy – "Honky Tonk Woman" or "I'm Through Crying Over You" – and he was one of the many who not only inspired Elvis, but helped him learn the guitar and piano.

WHEN ELVIS WAS TWELVE, Slim occasionally let him perform on his shows.

BY THIS TIME ELVIS was singing "Old Shep" all over the place, including outside the Tupelo hotel for cash. His singing of the maudlin tale so affected his fifth grade teacher, Mrs Grimes, that she almost broke down in tears. Instead of doing so, she made Elvis repeat the performance for the school principal, Mr Cole,

Elvis' first performances took place on the back of flat-top trucks and in small clubs and auditoriums where the audience could get a good look at his exotically handsome features. The excitement of the mostly female audiences was only increased when Elvis cut loose (right). Bill Black is playing bass behind him.

who was so impressed he entered Elvis for the children's talent contest in the 1945 Mississippi-Alabama Fair and Dairy Show, held annually at Tupelo's fairground. After singing "Old Shep," the ten-year-old Elvis walked off with the second prize of five dollars and free admission to the rides.

IN JANUARY 1946, GLADYS bought him his first guitar at the Tupelo Hardware Company for $7.75 (often quoted as $12.75). Vernon's brother, Lester, had married Gladys' sister, Cletus, and he also helped Elvis to learn the guitar. At the same time, Elvis was getting free piano lessons from his uncles, Johnny and Vester, the preacher Frank Smith and, of course, Mississippi Slim.

Mother, father and son (below), before Gladys succumbed to illness caused by stress and secret drinking.

"I DON'T DO NO DIRTY BODY MOVEMENTS. WHEN I SING I JUST START JUMPING. IF I STAND STILL I'M DEAD. I AIN'T GOT NO DEFINITION OF ROCK 'N' ROLL."
Elvis

THOUGH ELVIS WOULD ALWAYS be fixed in people's minds with the guitar, the piano was in fact his first love.

ON THE OTHER HAND, a guitar was easier to carry, so when the family moved to the outskirts of Shakerag and Elvis had to change schools, he made the long walk to his new school, Milam, barefooted, wearing dungarees, and with his guitar slung across his shoulder.

HE TOOK EVERY OPPORTUNITY to sing at Milam school. According to his homeroom teacher, Mrs Camp, he was good enough to silence the other kids when he did so. He also stirred up a lot of resentment and had to learn to defend himself. He refused to stop singing and often informed the other kids that he would one

"GIRLS ARE WONDERFUL. GIRLS ARE THE GREATEST AND MOSTEST AND LOVELIEST. ANYBODY THAT SAYS HE DOESN'T LIKE GIRLS IS MISSING HIS LIFE. THERE WOULDN'T BE ANYTHING WITHOUT GIRLS."
Elvis Presley, October 29, 1956

day play the *Grand Ole Opry*. Though otherwise shy, he pursued the girls a lot and refused to take "No" for an answer.

THE OTHER KIDS CALLED Elvis "white trash" because his family was poor, his house had no porch, and his father had gone to prison. Nevertheless, he took his pride from his music and went his own unique way.

FROM HIS PARENTS, THE guitar-playing preacher Frank Smith, and his regular attendances at church, Elvis learned gospel music. From Mississippi Slim and the many other musicians and singers on Radio WELO and the "Saturday Jamboree," he learned country music. From other music stations he learned about Dean Martin

"ELVIS HAS BEEN DESCRIBED VARIOUSLY AS A BARITONE AND A TENOR. AN EXTRAORDINARY COMPASS AND A VERY WIDE RANGE OF VOCAL COLOR HAVE SOMETHING TO DO WITH THIS DIVERGENCE OF OPINION."
Henry Pleasants, *The Great American Popular Singers*

Elvis' controversial body movements (left) were in fact picked up from the physically active gospel preachers of the Holiness churches he attended in childhood, then embellished with the gestures of the black performers he had seen on Beale Street. Soon a gospel group, the Jordanaires (above), were on the road with Elvis.

29

and similar crooners. In 1947, when he moved with his family first to Mulberry Alley, then to 1010 North Green Street, on the edge of Shakerag, he was exposed for the first time to "black" music.

HE WOULD EXPERIENCE EVEN more of the latter when, in 1948, the family moved to Memphis.

THE PRESLEYS SPENT THEIR first year in Memphis in a boarding house in Washington Avenue, then moved into a cockroach-infested four-story house at 572 Poplar Avenue, near the downtown commercial section of North Memphis. The following year they moved into a low rent housing project, the Lauderdale Courts, a two-bedroom, ground floor apartment run by the Memphis Housing Authority and located at 185 Winchester Street.

IN HIS FIRST YEAR in Memphis Elvis went to Christine School on Third Street, then later moved over to the bigger L.C. Humes High School in Manasas Street, North Memphis. Contrary to the widely accepted view of the young Elvis as an uneducated "truck driver" type, he was well educated at Humes High and, at the urging of his mother, took every opportunity to better himself. While majoring in history and English, his other activities included membership of the Reserve Officers' Training Corps, English club, speech club, history club, and biology club. He also worked in his spare time in the library.

AT HUMES HIGH, HE became friends with George Klein, the president of his class, and with another pupil, Red West. Klein would become a member of Elvis' entourage during the early tours and remain a trusted friend to the very end. Red West would later become a member of the "Memphis Mafia" and gain a controversial reputation for his part in the writing of the widely despised book, *Elvis: What Happened?* (1977).

BY HIS SIXTEENTH YEAR, Elvis was already very handsome. His dark, Valentino good looks were rendered exotic by his Indian ancestry and slightly curled upper lip. The shy good-looker made himself even more noticeable with his brilliantined hair, pompadour at the front, duck-tailed at the back (like Captain Marvel) and by wearing unusually colorful clothes, strongly favoring pink.

THIS DISTINCTIVE (SOME WOULD SAY "HOODLUM") appearance gained him a lot of attention, much of it unpleasant. Just as Elvis' singing at school in Tupelo had caused jealously and resentment, so too did his gaudy appearance at Humes High. Again, he had to brave ridicule and defend himself with his fists, which he did with alarming regularity for an otherwise shy, well-mannered boy.

THE PRESLEY FAMILY LIVED just above the poverty line, supported by Vernon's paycheck from the United Paint Company. To supplement their inadequate income, Gladys took on anything she could find, from cafeteria worker to nurse's aid in St. Joseph's Hospital. She also started drinking heavily. This made her put on weight and lose her slim appearance for all time.

AS PROTECTIVE OF HIS mother as she was of him, Elvis helped out by mowing

"A BLACK SINGER WILL JUMP THE BEAT, GET BEHIND THE BEAT, AND ELVIS WOULD DO ALL THAT NATURALLY. YOU KNOW, WITH BLACK SINGERS IT'S LIKE WRINGING A DISHRAG, GETTING ALL THE WATER OUT OF IT, THEY TAKE A WORD AND DO THE SAME THING. ELVIS COULD DO MORE WITH ONE WORD THAN ANY OTHER MAN I HEARD SING."
J.D. Sumner

30

lawns and working every evening as a cinema usher in Lowes State Theater. The latter did not last long, however, as he was soon fired for punching out a fellow employee. He also worked the night-shift at the Marl Metal Products Company, but was forced to quit when he began suffering from fatigue.

ON JANUARY 7, 1953, when Elvis had just turned eighteen, the Presleys left the housing project and moved in with relatives in Cypress Avenue. By April they had moved back to their old neighborhood, renting their own apartment at 462 Alabama Street.

BY THIS TIME, ELVIS was listening to Radio WDIA, the Memphis station that constantly pumped out the hits of B.B. King, Rufus Thomas, Joe Hill Lewis and other leading black rhythm and blues performers. He had also started exploring Beale Street.

BEALE STREET, OR MEMPHIS 42nd Street, the "Home of the Blues," was filled with honky-tonks, hookers, drug peddlers, and great black musicians. Though supposedly over-protected by his mother, Elvis often went there after school to buy flashy clothes, mostly at Lasky Brothers on the corner of Second and Beale Streets. He also went there to see the performers in the black clubs – and he often performed with them.

ELVIS WAS FIRST EXPOSED to black music when he lived close to Shakerag, in Tupelo, and listened to the tambourine, guitar and piano music emanating from the Sanctified Church services. The Presleys were widely known to respect the blacks, and Elvis got to know the Shakerag community more intimately when he helped his black truck-driver friend, John Allen Cooke, deliver groceries for Brown's Store on Gloster Street, next to Milam. So Elvis was well prepared for Beale Street when he went there to observe and perform.

ROBERT HENRY, THE BEALE STREET promoter who often took Elvis to watch the colored singers, believes that Elvis got his wiggle from Charlie Burse, or Ukulele Ike, who performed in the Gray Mule and the Hotel Improvement Club.

AMONG THOSE WHOM ELVIS saw perform in the black clubs was Roy Brown, the rhythm and blues singer-songwriter who penned "Good Rockin' Tonight," which Elvis loved and would soon record for Sam Phillips. Another Beale Street performer who strongly influenced him was the legendary blues guitarist, singer and songwriter B.B. King, who was then recording on the predominantly "black" Sun label. As Elvis' subsequent recording career would show clearly, he was also in love with the work of Arthur "Big Boy" Crudup, Chuck Berry and Little Richard, who were then recording many of their classic songs.

NAT D. WILLIAMS, NEWSPAPER columnist, DJ, Beale Street's unofficial mayor, and emcee at the Palace Amateur Nights, has confirmed that Elvis not only visited Beale Street clubs on a regular basis, but also performed in them with the black musicians. According to Williams, Elvis sang the blues not quite like a black man, but not like a white man either. He "had something in between that made the blues

Elvis could look angelic (below) or demonic (right). These contradictions only seemed to make him more appealing.

"WE HAD ONE OF THOSE RADIOS BUILT IN TO THE WALL OF OUR SITTING ROOM AT THE TIME, AND SUDDENLY I HEARD THIS MAGICIAN'S VOICE COMING OUT OF IT. THE EFFECT WAS COMPLETELY MAGICAL – AS IF THERE WAS A GENIE SITTING THERE BESIDE THE WALL."
Irene Handl, actress and novelist

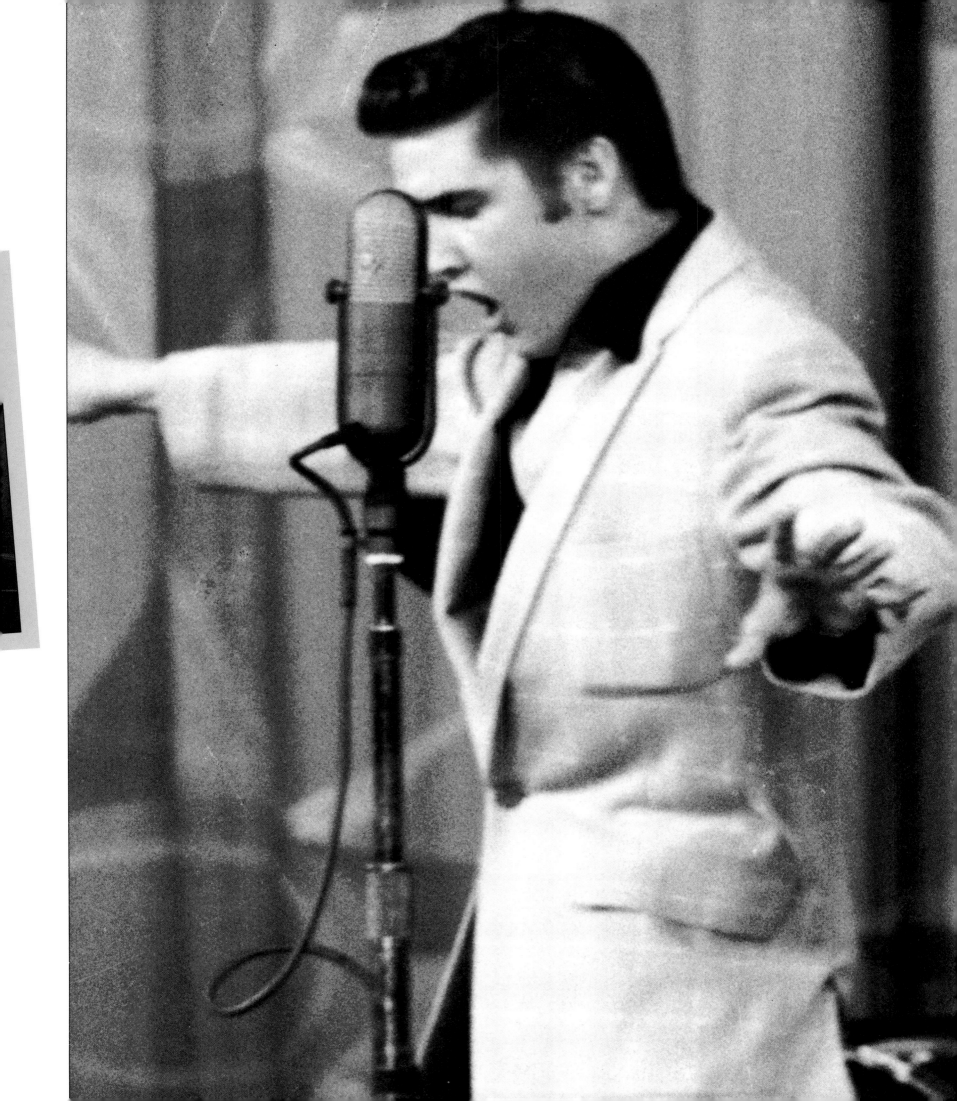

sort of different." The black audiences, Williams says, were "crazy" about him.

ELVIS WAS CERTAINLY OPEN enough about this. "The colored folks," he told the *Charlotte Observer* on June 26, 1956, "been singing it and playing it just like I'm doin' now, man, for more years than I know. They played it like that in the shanties and in their juke joints and nobody paid it no mind 'til I goosed it up. I got it from them. Down in Tupelo, Mississippi, I used to hear old Arthur Crudup bang his box the way I do now, and I said if I ever got to the place I could feel all old Arthur felt, I'd be a music man like nobody ever saw."

ELVIS WAS NOT ONLY singing the blues in Beale Street, but already causing riots when he did so. According to Williams, when Elvis performed at a particular Beale Street benefit show, about a thousand "black, brown and beige teenage girls in the audience" created a "wild crescendo of sound" and "took off like scalded cats in the direction of Elvis …. It took some time and several white cops to quell the melee and protect Elvis."

FURTHER PROOF THAT ELVIS was already a "natural" came with the high school talent contest during his senior year, when he performed "Cold, Cold Icy Fingers" and "Old Shep" to an audience of 1,600 pupils. According to former pupil Martha Wallace, the girl beside her was so moved by Elvis' singing that she fainted. Elvis' homeroom teacher has stated that the song was greeted with "pandemonium" and Elvis came off the stage, saying, "They really liked me, Miss Scrivener. They really liked me."

ON MAY 26, 1953, he hitchhiked the 240 miles to Meridian, Mississippi, carrying his guitar, to take part in the talent contest at the first Jimmy Rodgers "The Father of Country Music" Festival. (Rodgers was the singer so beloved by Gladys Presley.) Again, Elvis won second prize.

GRADUATING LATER IN THE year, he went to work for the Precision Tool Factory. This didn't last long and soon he was working as a $1.25-an-hour truck driver for the Crown Electric Company, located at 353 Poplar Avenue, Memphis.

IN THE SUMMER OF 1953 Elvis was dating Dixie Locke. He was also seeing Barbara Hearn, a young lady of refined beauty and good background. Dixie would give him up when he began touring with Scotty Moore and Bill Black. Barbara Hearne, who was hoping to marry him, lost him when the touring became intensive and took him away too much.

BUT BY 1953 ELVIS was intent on cutting a record. Some time in the fall he walked into Sam Phillips' Memphis Record Service at 706 Union Street to record "My Happiness" and "That's When Your Heartaches Begin."

BOTH SONGS HAD BEEN hits for a black group known as the Ink Spots.

IN 1953 SAM PHILLIPS was already well on the road to becoming one of the most influential figures in popular music. Born in Florence, Alabama, in 1935, his fascination with black music began when he was a child and heard the "blues" of the blacks working the fields. After working as a DJ at various stations in Alabama and Nashville, he moved to Nashville in 1946 and worked at WREC. Eventually, he founded the Memphis Recording Service, located at 706 Union Avenue, where he defied local prejudice by recording mainly black artists and selling the masters to Chess Records in Chicago. He recorded, among others, B.B. King, Chester "Howlin Wolf" Burnett, Walter Horton, Bobby Bland, Little Junior Parker, Rufus Thomas, and the Johnny Burnett Trio. In 1952 he founded Sun Records in the same building and hired Marion Keisker, a former "Miss Radio" of Memphis, to work for him. When Elvis first walked into the building to cut "My Happiness" it was Miss Keisker who had the honor of greeting him.

Elvis could never start recording without first getting "in the mood" by singing gospel songs, fooling around on the drums, or playing the piano. While he occasionally played piano on his records, he generally left it to famed session-men such as Floyd Cramer and Dudley Brooks. The latter is seen with Elvis (right) in the studio at RCA New York, circa 1957.

LEGEND HAS IT THAT Elvis wanted to record "My Happiness" as a birthday present for his mother, but this seems unlikely as the record was cut a few months later. Another explanation makes more sense.

FOR YEARS IT WAS believed that Sam Phillips introduced Elvis to guitarist Scotty Moore and bass player Bill Black at the first Sun sessions in 1954. However, Elaine Dundy's reliable research shows that the three first met in 1951, when Elvis was sixteen. At that time Scotty and Bill were members of a country band called

The very first Elvis recording was "My Happiness," which he cut at the Sun Studios, Memphis, in the summer of 1954, possibly as a birthday present for his mother. Originally on a $4, ten-inch acetate, it was lost for thirty-seven years and was finally released on an official RCA compilation album in 1991. However, the first professional recording was "That's All Right [Mama]," released on the Sun label on July 19, 1954. It became a local hit and started Elvis on the road to worldwide fame.

the Starlight Wranglers, which was led by Doug Poindexter. This band had not only played professionally around Memphis for some time, but had already recorded for Sam Phillips in 1950, backing Johnny Burnett and others.

BILL BLACK FIRST MET Elvis in 1951, when he went to Lauderdale Court to visit his widowed mother, Ruby Black, who was a friend of Gladys and had two sons who went to school with Elvis. Bill picked Elvis as a potential talent the minute he heard him sing in the yard of Lauderdale Courts, and soon he and Elvis were jamming together. Bill introduced Elvis to Scotty Moore, and as early as 1952 was urging him to cut a demonstration record at the Memphis Recording Service. Shyness probably prevented Elvis from doing so until 1953, when he may have used his mother's so-called "birthday" as an excuse or the means of working up the courage. Certainly Elvis is clear about his motives.

"I WENT TO SUN, paid my four bucks to the lady because I had a notion to find out what I really sounded like. I had been singing all my life and I was kind of curious."

WHEN HE HEARD HIMSELF on the acetate, he wasn't pleased, describing the results as "terrible … like someone beating on a bucket lid." Luckily, Marion Keisker thought more highly of him; so much so that she decided to tape him.

"OVER AND OVER I remember Sam saying, 'If I could find a white man who had the Negro sound and the Negro feel, I could make a million dollars.' This is what I heard in Elvis, this ... what I guess they now call 'soul,' this Negro sound. So I taped it. I wanted Sam to know."

PHILLIPS WASN'T INITIALLY IMPRESSED, but Elvis returned to the Memphis Recording Service on January 4, 1954, to record "Casual Love Affair" and "I'll Never Stand in Your Way" on a ten-inch acetate for $4. During this visit he met Sam Phillips for the first time. Sam was impressed enough to take down his address and telephone number, but another six months would pass before, at the behest of Marion Keisker, he formally took Elvis on as one of his artists.

SAM NEEDED SOMEONE TO record "Without You" and Marion Keisker recommended Elvis. Elvis couldn't get to grips with the song, but when the disappointed Phillips asked him what he could sing, the response was, "I can sing anything."

WHEN ELVIS THEN PROVED it by running through a collection of songs covering gospel, the blues, country, old standards and some Dean Martin styled popular hits, Sam was impressed enough to put him together with Scotty Moore and Bill Black to rehearse for some proper recording sessions.

THEY DID NOT REHEARSE at Sun, but at Scotty Moore's house, where over a lengthy period they developed and polished the sound they wanted.

IN OTHER WORDS, CONTRARY to popular belief, they had already created their unique fusion of country music and rhythm and blues when they entered the Sun Studio to cut their first record.

THE FIRST SUN STUDIO recording sessions with Scotty Moore on electric guitar, Bill Black on upright bass, and Elvis on rhythm guitar, took place on the evening of July 5, 1954. The first song attempted was "I Love You Because," an anguished country weeper with a spoken bridge. On the second take, they cut the spoken bridge, added a whistled introduction, and performed with more confidence. They tried it twice more, but one take was not completed and the fourth version would not be released.

AFTER THAT, THEY TURNED off the tapes and tried "some of those country-oriented things." None of them came to much – certainly they weren't taped – but then Elvis suggested trying Arthur Crudup's "That's All Right [Mama]." When Elvis cut into it, singing high and loose, Scotty Moore and Bill Black followed suit. Sam Phillips turned on the tapes, made them run through it again, and that was it.

THE VOICE ON "That's All Right [Mama]" is high, urgent, sensual and as free as a bird: a "black" voice with "white" intonations. The track is pure Beale Street blues with a pounding bass rhythm, yet Scotty Moore's guitar retains a country flavor. It is exactly, to the very last note, what Sam Phillips had wanted.

THE GREAT BLUEGRASS NUMBER "Blue Moon of Kentucky" was cut four days later. The first version was a brief, medium-tempo, country rocker with a strong

"OUTSIDE OUR HOUSE, IT WAS LIKE BACKSTAGE THE NIGHT BEFORE – PANDEMONIUM. THE GIRLS HAD SPOTTED ELVIS' CAR THERE AND THEY CAME CHARGING IN – WE COULDN'T STOP 'EM. THEY SAW BY THE BEDCLOTHES HE'D BEEN SLEEPING ON OUR SOFA AND I COULDN'T BELIEVE MY EYES BUT THEY RIPPED THAT SOFA TO PIECES – IT WAS NOTHING BUT A WOODEN FRAME BY THE TIME THEY WERE FINISHED."
Buddy Bain, Tupelo TV producer

and assured vocal treatment. At the end of it, Scotty ran humorously down the chords, Elvis took a nervous breath, and Sam Phillips, with a laugh, said, "Fine, man! Hell, that's *different!* That's a pop song!" But they taped another, much faster version, with an extraordinarily driving, eccentric vocal by Elvis that turned the whole thing inside-out and made it something unique.

SAM PHILLIPS PICKED THAT cut as the flip-side to "That's All Right [Mama]."

"ON ONE SIDE WE had a country and western ballad with a rhythm and blues feel, on the other side we had a strictly rhythm and blues song with a slight country feel to it."

Memphis Radio WLVS disc jockey George Klein was Elvis' buddy at Humes High School and remained a close, trusted friend to the very end.

The strain of unprecedented fame was already showing in Elvis' mother and would soon be visible in him, but between 1954 and 1956, when these photographs were taken, Elvis was clearly feeling as free as a bird and was all set to soar high. He was enjoying himself.

BOTH SONGS WERE RELEASED as a single on July 19. However, the single was given a great boost even before its release when, on the evening of July 7, Dewey Phillips featured "That's All Right [Mama]" on his WHBQ show "Red, Hot and Blue," which had a black and white audience interested in rhythm and blues. At about the same time, DJ John Lepley was playing the flip side, "Blue Moon of Kentucky," on his WHHM Memphis program, devoted to country music.

WITH BOTH SIDES OF the single being played, one on a rhythm and blues program, the other on a country program, it soon sold over 20,000 copies and put Elvis on the road to unprecedented success.

The King of Rock-and-Roll

"They all think I'm a sex maniac. They're all frustrated old types, anyway. I'm just natural."

Elvis Presley

O N JULY 12, 1954, on the advice of Sam Phillips, Scotty Moore signed Elvis to a year's contract as part of the trio, with fifty percent to Elvis, and twenty-five percent each to Scotty and Bill. The following Monday, July 19, Elvis' first single, "That's All Right [Mama]," was released. By the end of the month, it was number three in the Memphis country and western chart.

BOB NEAL, A RADIO WMPS Memphis DJ and agent, booked Elvis for his historically important show at the Overton Park Shell, Memphis, on July 30. At that show Elvis became an overnight sensation by using his uninhibited body movements while singing "Good Rockin' Tonight." The girls shrieked and wriggled so much that Webb Pierce, the upstaged headliner, hissed "sonofabitch!" The hysteria was repeated when Elvis made his second appearance at the Overton Park Shell on August 10.

CALLING THEMSELVES THE Blue Moon Boys, Elvis, Scotty and Bill hit the road. Early gigs in Memphis after the release of the first Sun single included the Airways Shopping Center, where they first performed on a flat-bed truck; the Eagle's Nest, a ballroom on Lamar Avenue; the Bel Air Club, where in 1954 Scotty and Bill had played with the Starlight Wranglers; and the Airport Inn. It was at the latter that Oscar Davis was supposed to have first seen Elvis perform and relayed the news back to his boss, Colonel Tom Parker.

DURING THE SAME YEAR, Elvis was booked by Jim Denny to play the "Grand Ole Opry," the country music show broadcast on WSM Radio from the Ryman Auditorium in Nashville and widely known as the Mecca of Country Music. He appeared on September 25, two days after the release of his second Sun single, "Good Rockin' Tonight" and "I Don't Care if the Sun Don't Shine," but after his

"I DON'T LIKE THEM PULLING MY CLOTHES AND WRITING ON MY CHEEKS IN LIPSTICK AND WANTING ME TO KISS THEM. I DON'T SEE ANY SENSE FOR THEM TO DANCE A ROCK-AND-ROLL ON THE HOOD OF MY CAR OR DRIVE A KNIFE INTO THE UPHOLSTERY. BUT SOME DO IT, AND LOOK AT ME WITH THE QUEEREST LOOK IN THEIR EYES WHILE THEY'RE DOING IT. THAT PART KIND OF FRIGHTENS ME."
Elvis Presley, October 29, 1956

performance Denny almost broke his heart by telling him to go back to driving a truck.

THE FOLLOWING MONTH, ON October 16, Elvis made the first of many appearances on the "Louisiana Hayride," the Saturday night country show broadcast on KWKH radio from Shreveport, Louisiana. Elvis, now being billed under his own name, was paid eighteen dollars a show, Scotty and Bill twelve dollars each. Elvis appeared regularly until December the following year. This included his appearance on the "Louisiana Hayride" TV show of March 5, 1955. The resident "Louisiana Hayride" drummer, J.D. Fontana, became Elvis' regular studio drummer and joined Scotty Moore and Bill Black onstage.

IN JANUARY 1955 ELVIS' third Sun single, "Milkcow Blues Boogie" – an extraordinary performance of a straight blues – coupled with the country and western foot-tapper, "You're a Heartbreaker," became another local hit. But his fourth single, "Baby, Let's Play House," issued on April 1, took off in June when the media informed the whole country that in Jackson, Florida, Elvis' shirt, jacket and even shoes had been ripped off by hysterical teenage fans.

"BABY, LET'S PLAY HOUSE" was Elvis' breakthrough record.

HE PLAYED IN AMORY, Mississippi, in 1955 with Johnny Cash and Carl Perkins. (The latter reputedly penned his rockabilly masterpiece, "Blue Suede Shoes,"

In 1954 Elvis was still touring with a combo consisting of himself on rhythm guitar, the legendary Scotty Moore on lead guitar, and Bill Black on upright bass. Drummer J.D. Fontana was added to the group in 1955, and soon the Jordanaires were adding vocal back-up. Bill Black and one of the Jordanaires can be seen below, in a photo taken during Elvis' performance on the "Louisiana Hayride" television show of March 5, 1955. By this time Elvis had toured with many of the top country performers, including Johnny Cash (right). Reportedly, it was while playing with Elvis and Cash in Amory, Mississippi, in 1955, that Carl Perkins penned "Blue Suede Shoes," which would soon become another Elvis hit and instant classic.

"HE WAS ONE OF THE MOST PHENOMENALLY CONSISTENT PERFORMERS. RARELY DID A TAKE FLAG DOWN OR DROP IN ENERGY. HE'D PREFER ONE TAKE BECAUSE OF A CERTAIN NOTE HE HIT OR A TURN OF PHRASE, BUT THEY WERE ALL GOOD."
Jerry Leiber, songwriter

when staying with Elvis and Johnny Cash at the Roadside Inn, Amory.) Country singer June Carter was part of local impresario Colonel Parker's talent stable in 1955, and toured briefly with Elvis. Elvis also appeared with the Carter Sisters and Marty Robbins.

BY NOW, BECAUSE OF his unique way of combining rhythm and blues with country and western, as well as his uninhibited stage act, Elvis was being called "The Boppin' Hillbilly," "The Hillbilly Cat," "The King of Western Bop," and "The Memphis Flash." He was also causing hysteria wherever he appeared and clearly enjoying it.

THEN COLONEL TOM PARKER entered his life.

THE BACKGROUND TO Thomas A. Parker is still shrouded in mystery, but he was probably born as Andreas Cornelius van Juijk in Breda, Holland on June 26, 1909. He entered the United States in 1929, perhaps illegally, by jumping ship, and never took up American nationality. Instead, he legitimized himself by adopting an English name and enlisting in the army. At Fort Barrancas, Pensacola Harbor, Florida, where he was stationed, he picked up his famous Southern accent. After

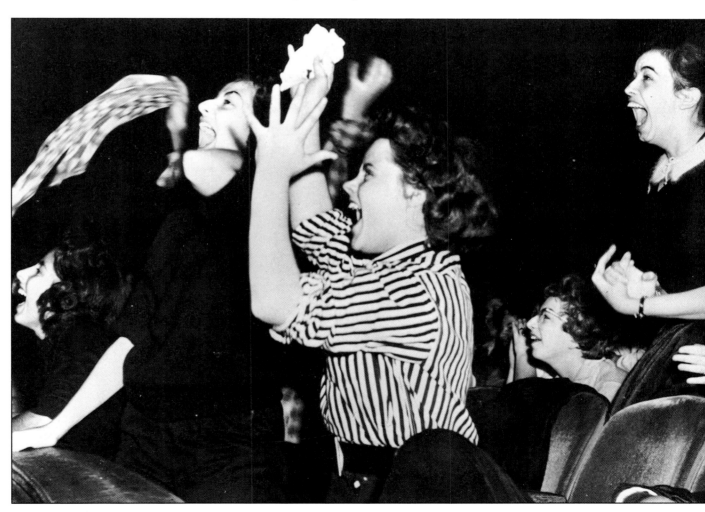

A combination of dark, Valentino good looks, sideburns, pompadour, flashy clothes, and uninhibited body movements continued to excite and delight the girls in 1956.

49

completing his term, he took work with a series of carnivals, selling donkey rides, telling fortunes, and charging cherry-soda bottle-tops for admission to his "monkey-and-pony" act. While with the Royal American Show in Tampa, Florida, Parker met and married the former Mrs Marie Ross née Mott, whom he promptly nicknamed "Miz Rie," or "misery."

DURING HIS YEARS WITH the carnivals, Parker developed his promotional and negotiating talents, as well as his "loveable rogue" or "carny man," persona. At some point, he became the head dog catcher of Tampa, Florida, and made extra money from it by creating an animal cemetery, with proper caskets, funeral services, flowers and ornate gravestones.

THIS WAS FOLLOWED BY a brief period as singer Gene Austin's manager. When a dissatisfied Austin split, Parker became a front man for the *Grand Ole Opry* traveling tent show, which starred singer Eddy Arnold. Gradually, Parker took over the management of Arnold, whose name attracted other acts. An old carny friend then persuaded Governor Jimmy Davis to make Parker an honorary "Colonel" of Louisiana. Another spurious colonelship was wrangled from Tennessee Governor Frank C. Clement. Thus promoted, Parker was then demoted by Eddie Arnold, who fired him. Parker was also rumored to be involved in the selling of the drug Hadacol until it was banned in various states.

UNDETERRED, PARKER WAS SOON managing another country singer, Hank Snow, while strengthening his ties with RCA Records, and Hill and Range Music Publishers. By this time he had gained a reputation as a practical joker, born gambler, con man and stubborn negotiator – or, in the words of Elvis biographer Jerry Hopkins – "a combination of W.C. Fields and P.T. Barnum." Unfortunately, he was also a manager whose ideas for promotion were based on his circus background.

IN 1954 BOB NEAL, a DJ at the radio station WMPS, Memphis, made a lot of bookings for Elvis. In December of that year he took over Elvis' management, forming a company called Elvis Presley Enterprises. By then, Colonel Parker and Hank Snow were running the *Hank Snow Jamboree Attractions*, a touring show with many leading country artists. The Colonel began booking Elvis for the show early in 1955, and could not have failed to know when Elvis became the main draw. Bob Neal and Colonel Parker met to discuss Elvis during the latter's Big D Jamboree performance in Dallas, Texas, on June 24, 1955. Subsequently, on August 15, after singer Hank Snow had personally aroused the interest of RCA, Colonel Parker signed Elvis to a contract that would, against all normal standards of practice, bind the singer to him for life.

SAM PHILLIPS KNEW THAT Elvis was becoming too big for him to handle, so on November 22 he sold Elvis' contract and master tapes to RCA for a total of $35,000: the biggest fee ever paid to a country and western artist. Sam and Elvis both profited by the deal. Sam went on to produce Jerry Lee Lewis, Roy Orbison,

"ELVIS PRESLEY CREATED PANDEMONIUM AMONG THE TEENAGE COUNTRY FANS IN JACKSONVILLE, FLA., RECENTLY, AND BEFORE HE COULD BE RESCUED FROM HIS SWOONING ADMIRERS, THEY HAD RELIEVED HIM OF HIS TIE, HANDKERCHIEFS, BELT, AND THE GREATER PART OF HIS COAT AND SHIRT."
Billboard, 1955

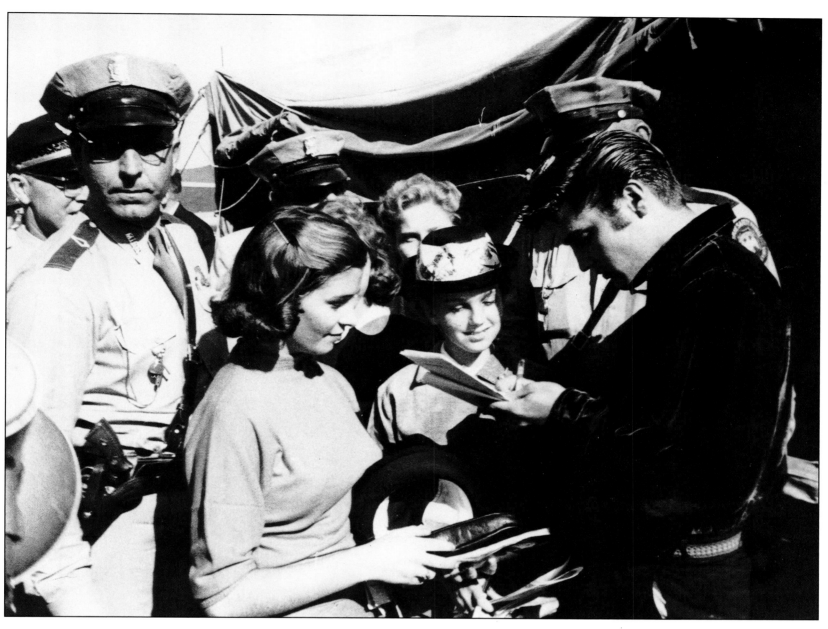

In 1956 Elvis returned in triumph to Tupelo, the town of his birth, to sing again in the Mississippi-Alabama Fair where he had first performed as a child. Left: an amused Scotty Moore keeps playing behind a fooling Elvis. Above: the Memphis Flash is protected by police while signing autographs before the show and (right) the concert is interrupted while another hysterical girl is led off the stage. Many other girls fainted with excitement before the show ended.

52

When Elvis moved from Sun to RCA in 1956, his recordings were masterminded by the distinguished producer Steve Sholes (below). Though Elvis was undoubtedly his own creative master, it may have been Sholes who encouraged him to try for a fuller, more produced sound. This he did by adding the vocal back-up and hand-clapping of the Jordanaires (bottom right), seen here with Elvis at the Tupelo-Mississippi State Fair, and supplementing guitarist Scotty Moore, bass player Bill Black and drummer J.D. Fontana with pianists Floyd Cramer and Dudley Brooks. At first Elvis shared the same room as the other musicians, but his inability to stop stomping his feet forced Sholes to isolate him in a separate recording booth.

Carl Perkins, Charlie Rich, and Johnny Cash. Meanwhile, Elvis moved to RCA to make some of his finest recordings and become the most famous singer in history.

STEVE SHOLES WAS THE dedicated producer in charge of recording sessions when Elvis first moved to RCA. Sholes liked Elvis a lot, sensed what he wanted, and helped him to get it. Well-known session pianist Floyd Cramer created the distinctive piano styles on the early RCA tracks. These included "Heartbreak Hotel," recorded at Elvis' first session at RCA Nashville Studio, 1525 McGavock Street, on January 10, 1956. The track is notable not only for Elvis' extraordinarily dramatic, eccentric vocal, but also for Scotty Moore's blistering guitar solo and Floyd Cramer's blues-based piano break. Also in on the sessions as backing singers were Gordon Stoke, leader of the Jordanaires, a distinguished pop-gospel vocal group, and two of his singers, Ben and Brock Speer. The whole group would not be used until a later date.

53

AFTER LAYING DOWN SOME more tracks, including "I Was the One," "Money Honey," and "I Got a Woman," Elvis made his first national TV appearance on "The Dorsey Brothers Show" on January 28, singing "Blue Suede Shoes" and "Heartbreak Hotel." His performance resulted in a barrage of complaints from adults and appeals for more from the teenagers. Pleased, the producers invited Elvis back five more times. By the time of his sixth appearance, "Heartbreak Hotel" was number one in the charts and "Presleymania" had well and truly begun.

ELVIS KEPT CUTTING RECORDS. Two days after his first TV appearance he was in the RCA New York Studio for a session that included "My Baby Left Me." The second RCA New York Studio session, in February, included "Blue Suede Shoes," "Lawdy Miss Clawdy," "Tutti Frutti," "Shake, Rattle and Roll," and "One-Sided Love Affair." Elvis played the rollicking boogie piano solo on the latter.

LEGENDARY GUITARIST (SOON TO BE PRODUCER) Chet Atkins played with Scotty Moore on these sessions. Pianists Shorty Long and Dudley Moore sometimes stood in for Floyd Cramer. Yet, according to producer Steve Sholes, the timeless quality of the recordings was due to Elvis' relentless perfectionism. Another producer, Bones Howe, was in no doubt that Elvis was virtually producing his own records and doing things in the studio that had never been done before.

"TODAY EVERYBODY MAKES RECORDS that way," Bones told Jerry Hopkins. "Back then Elvis was the only one. He was the forerunner of everything that's record production these days. Consciously or unconsciously, everyone imitated him."

THAT MAY EXPLAIN WHY, WHEN twelve of those tracks were released on Elvis' first LP, *Elvis Presley*, the album went straight into Billboard's bestselling chart.

ON APRIL 1, 1956, Elvis made his screen test for producer Hal Wallis, performing opposite character actor Frank Faylen in a scene from the Broadway play, *The Rainmaker*, which Wallis was about to produce as a movie starring Burt Lancaster and Katherine Hepburn. Wallis was impressed, thinking Elvis a natural, and signed him to a non-exclusive, three-picture contract. Elvis would receive $100,000 for the first, $150,000 for the second, and $200,000 for the third.

IN AN INTERVIEW GIVEN to the *Waco News Tribune* on April 19, 1956, Elvis stated that he would be having a non-singing role in his first movie, also starring Burt Lancaster and Katherine Hepburn – obviously *The Rainmaker*. Unfortunately this did not come to pass. Though Wallis would later go on record as saying he believed Elvis to be a "genius", he did not put him into his more prestigious production, but instead scheduled him for *The Reno Brothers*, a low-budget Civil War western with a nondescript cast. This would be renamed *Love Me Tender*.

ON APRIL 3, TWO days after his screen test, Elvis made his second television appearance, this time on the "Milton Berle Show," singing "Heartbreak Hotel," "Money Honey," and "Blue Suede Shoes." On April 5 he appeared on the same show, performing "Hound Dog" and "I Want You, I Need You, I Love You."

Elvis' second album, Elvis *released in 1957, included a recording of his childhood prize-winner, "Old Shep," a blues number written by Arthur "That's All Right [Mama]" Crudup, three Little Richard hits, country material by Chet Atkins and Boudleaux Byrant, Leiber and Stoller's classic ballad, "Love Me," and another chart-topper, "Paralyzed." Though the album confirmed Elvis' mastery of most forms of popular music, he had already gone to Hollywood to make the first of his movies,* Love Me Tender. *Bottom and far left: test shots taken on location for that movie.*

LATER IN THE MONTH, from April 23 to 29, he performed nightly in the Venus Room of the New Frontier Hotel in Las Vegas. Elvis was thrilled to learn he would be earning $17,500 for the week. He was not so thrilled when he discovered that the middle-aged audience didn't quite know how to respond to him. He made up for this humiliation by having brief flings with Las Vegas showgirls Kitty Dolan and Kathy Gabriel.

A United Press copywriter described the Elvis shown here (right) as appearing "in the throes of ecstasy" as he prepared to make a live television appearance on "The Steve Allen Show" on October 28, 1956. In fact, Elvis looks super-cool, if not disdainful.

ON JULY 1, 1956, he appeared on "The Steve Allen Show," dressed up in a cowboy outfit for "Tumbleweed Presley," an inane skit with Steve Allen, Andy Griffith and comedienne Imogene Coca. He was allowed to wear his normal clothes for "I Want You, I Need You, I Love You," but Allen made him sing "Hound Dog" to a real hound dog, while dressed in ill-fitting tuxedo tails and bow-tie. Elvis took his revenge by grinning wickedly at the camera, patting the dog, then wiping his hand on his pants as if wiping the whole mess off.

NEXT DAY HE WAS back in the RCA New York Studios to compensate for his Las Vegas failure by making some of his finest recordings. The full contingent of

One of the few mistakes Elvis made in the early days was letting Steve Allen put him in "the tie and tails" for a notorious 1956 television appearance (above). His second mistake was appearing live to a middle-aged audience in Las Vegas the same year, but Liberace (above left) was supportive.

the bop-singing Jordanaires, including the previously absent Hoyt Hawkings (baritone), Neal Matthews (tenor) and Hugh Jarrett (bass), were introduced on the glorious "Don't be Cruel." Penned by Otis Blackwell and recorded on July 2, 1956, this was destined to be one of the biggest selling singles of all time. Sublime as it was, the track's flip-side was the classic "Hound Dog," which required thirty-one takes before Elvis was satisfied. With its savage guitar (Scotty Moore), machine-gun drumming (D.J. Fontana), staccato hand-clapping and background vocals (the Jordanaires) and, above all, with a sneering, challenging vocal by Elvis, "Hound Dog" went on to become a rock-and-roll anthem that paved the way for groups like the Rolling Stones.

NATIONWIDE FAME CAME ON September 9 with Elvis' first appearance on the all-important "The Sullivan Show," singing "Don't be Cruel," "Love Me Tender," "Reddy Teddy," and "Hound Dog." He returned on October 28 to sing virtually the same selection, only substituting "Love Me Tender" for "Reddy Teddy." The

Ed Sullivan (above) swore he would never have Elvis on his TV show, but the latter's growing fame soon made him relent. Later, Sullivan had nothing but praise for Elvis.

cameramen had been ordered to cut him off at the waist, but what he couldn't show he suggested with his broad grin, rolling eyes, and upper-body movements, so the girls screamed as loudly as ever.

THE SHOWS CAUSED A nationwide sensation and set the seal on Elvis' success. RCA capitalized on this by releasing fourteen songs, all taken from previously released Elvis LPs, on seven singles that sold over 100,000 copies each. The same week, "Hound Dog" was in the number one spot for the sixth week running; its flipside, "Don't be Cruel," was about to replace it, with both sides selling over two million copies each; and advance orders for the new single, "Love Me Tender," had reached 856,327 even before the record was shipped.

MOST OF THIS WAS due to Elvis' appearances on "The Sullivan Show." As Ed Sullivan had publicly vowed that he would never have Elvis on his show, this particular triumph must have made Elvis grin from ear to ear.

Elvis, guitarist Scotty Moore, bass player Bill Black, pianist Floyd Cramer, and drummer J.D. Fontana chat with actress Judy Tyler during the shooting of Elvis' third, and most controversial movie, Jailhouse Rock.

"I WAS A REAL LITTLE TODDLER WHEN I FIRST HEARD 'HOUND DOG.' I LEARNED TO PLAY DRUMS LISTENING TO HIM – BEATING ON TIN CANS TO HIS RECORDS."
Mick Fleetwood

60

THE TOURING CONTINUED AND was often a riot. Generally, Elvis hit the road with Scotty Moore, Bill Black, D.J. Fontana, Red West, rockabilly singer Cliff Gleaves, and two cousins, Junior and Gene Smith. They completed about 100,000 miles in that first year alone, covering most of the southern states. By this time the fans were fainting during Elvis' performances, hysterically fighting the police sent to guard him, tearing the clothes off his back and the shoes off his feet, demolishing his cars, and trying to get at him by climbing the fire-escapes of hotels or clambering through the rear windows of theaters.

THE CONTROVERSY OVER HIS stage act increased, troubling Elvis and causing anguish to his mother. The reviewer of his performance at the Fox Theater on May 25 described him as having "the profile of a Greek God and the motions of a Gilda Gray." He was also called "the Marlon Brando of the mountain-music set." After the first day of his two-day show at Jackson, Florida, Juvenile Court Judge Marion Gooding warned him to "keep it clean" and "remove his objectionable hip movements" from his act. (Elvis responded by wiggling his little finger instead, which drove the girls just as crazy.) On October 12, the *Dallas Morning News*, reviewing his Thursday evening appearance at the Cotton Bowl, talked of "gyrating pelvic motions which are best described as a cross between an Apache war dance and a burlesque queen's old-fashioned bumps and grind."

ELVIS PLEADED NOT GUILTY to all charges, though the strain of dealing with the constant accusations was beginning to show. On October 18 his "rebel" image was heightened when he became involved in a fight with two gas station attendants and floored both of them, including manager Ed Hopper. Elvis was called to court to give his side of the story, in the presence of Hopper, who had a black eye and bandaged eyebrow. Acquitted by Acting City Judge Sam Friedman, Elvis became even more of a hero to the young.

A FEW DAYS LATER, his second album, *Elvis*, raced up the bestseller charts. On this one, Elvis paid respect to his roots by including a blues by Arthur "Big Boy" Crudup and country material by Chet Atkins and Boudleaux Byrant. He also included his beloved "Old Shep" and three Little Richard hits, plus Leiber and Stoller's "Love Me" and Otis Blackwell's "Paralyzed," which became another million-selling single.

SINCE HE LOVED THE work of actor James Dean, Elvis was thrilled when, that same month, Natalie Wood, Dean's lovely young co-star in *Rebel without a Cause*, visited him in Memphis and went motorcycle riding with him and Nick Adams. According to actress Shelley Winters, Elvis and Natalie were deeply in love, but they were parted by the demands of their separate careers. Nevertheless, the romance between the *Rebel without a Cause* girl and the "King of rock-and-roll" began a global media obsession.

ON DECEMBER 4, PURE coincidence brought Elvis, Carl Perkins, Johnny Cash and Jerry Lee Lewis together in the Sun Recording Studio. Reputedly the four

Elvis' love life was always a topic of feverish speculation with the media, but never more so than when he became involved with Hollywood actress, Natalie Wood (right), shortly after she had co-starred with James Dean in the classic teen movie, Rebel without a Cause. *Nevertheless, the romance was short-lived.*

"I KNEW THEM BOTH VERY WELL AT THE TIME. NATALIE [WOOD] AND ELVIS WERE DEEPLY IN LOVE. AND IF THEY HAD BEEN ALLOWED TO MARRY, NONE OF THE REST OF IT WOULD HAVE HAPPENED!"
Shelley Winters, actress

jammed together, singing a mixture of gospel and pop songs, and Sam Phillips informally taped them. This unreleased tape would become legendary over the years as the "Million Dollar Session," but when it was finally released many years later, the so-called Million Dollar Quartet did not feature Johnny Cash and failed to make a million dollars. It was, however, a great and good-humored jamming session, featuring Elvis, Jerry Lee Lewis and Carl Perkins, with Elvis well to the fore. A true collector's item.

THE FIRST ELVIS PRESLEY National Fan Club was founded in the United States in 1957 by Kay Wheeler of Dallas, Texas, who later recounted her colorful experiences in an unpublished manuscript, *Growing Up with the Memphis Flash*. Before the year was out there were many more clubs and a total membership of approximately 250,000. The British Fan Club, which was to become the biggest and best in the world, was formed in August 1957 by Jeanne Saward and Dug Surtees. Within two years, the multiplying fan clubs would have a global membership of millions.

A photo of Elvis with Jerry Lee Lewis, Carl Perkins and Johnny Cash recording together in the Sun Studios (left) led to much speculation about a "Million Dollar Quartet." The released album, however, did not include Johnny Cash.

AWARE OF THIS, COLONEL PARKER licensed the Beverly Hills marketing firm of Howard Bell and Hank Saperstein, Special Products Inc., to exploit Elvis' name and likeness in every conceivable way, By the end of the first year, the estimated gross for this company's "Presleyana" was estimated at $55 million.

UNFORTUNATELY, WHILE MAKING A fortune for all concerned, Colonel Parker's promotions also ensured that Elvis was treated by respectable society more like a tawdry circus act than a remarkable, innovatory singer. By 1956 Parker's Special Products Inc had swamped the globe in Elvis shirts, slacks, underwear, socks, shoes, sweaters, bracelets, belts, ties, hats, T-shirts, 'kerchiefs, stuffed dogs, dolls, greeting cards, bubble gum cards, pins, pens, pencils, buttons, pillows, combs, bookends, photographs that lit up in the dark, even colognes and lipsticks (Hound Dog Orange, Heartbreak Hotel Pink, Tutti Frutti Red) and, naturally, guitars. Another Parker stunt was to have the Hollywood costume firm, Nudie's, make Elvis the $10,000 gold lamé tuxedo which he wears on the cover of the 1959 LP, *50,000,000 Elvis Fans Can't be Wrong*. (This tux has long been identified with Elvis, but in reality he only wore it for a few shows, then discarded

One of Colonel Parker's stunts was to have Elvis perform in a gold lamé tuxedo designed by the Hollywood costume firm, Nudie's. Elvis soon discarded it as being too hot and heavy, but later wore a lighter gold lamé jacket with black pants. The original gold lamé suit is the one used on the cover of the 1959 LP, 50,000,000 Elvis Fans Can't be Wrong. Below: Elvis with Nudie.

it because it was too heavy and hot.) Parker was also advertising his "merchandise" (his description of Elvis, not the products) with elephants and midgets (the Elvis Presley Midget Fan Club), and pandering to the media's response to him.

BY NOW ELVIS WAS being called "Mr. Wiggle & Shake," "Sir Swivelhips," "King of Rhythm," "The Blue Suede Bopper," "The Hip King," "Elvis the Pelvis," and, of course, "The King of rock-and-roll." Though his every remark at the time revealed him to be good-humored, perceptive, self-aware and tolerant, he was described as "morally insane" and "an inspiration for low IQ hoodlums" who "ought to be entertaining in the State Reformatory." In the rush to condemn him, his education was forgotten and his innovatory talents ignored. Instead, he was viewed as a "white trash" hoodlum who was purveying "animalistic nigger bop" to respectable white children. Colonel Parker contributed to the assault by referring to Elvis as "a wiggle machine" who could "go back to driving a truck" if he faded away.

ELVIS' FIRST MOVIE BEGAN shooting in August, 1956. Those expecting a rock-and-roll movie were in for disappointment. *Love Me Tender* is the story of three brothers who, not knowing that the Civil War has just ended, rob a Union depot,

then return to their farm to learn that Debra Paget, who was to have married the eldest brother (Richard Egan) has married the younger brother (Elvis) in the mistaken belief that Egan had been killed. Complications caused by the robbery and Paget's love for both men lead to a tragic ending, with Elvis dying in the arms of his brother and wife as his ghostly image sings the title song.

SHOT IN BLACK AND WHITE, the film is well mounted, but fails to rise above its "B" movie plot. What matters is that the young Elvis, if clearly an inexperienced actor, has undeniable screen presence and practically burns up the screen when he sings his four country songs. Invariably, his gyrations during "Poor Boy" and "Let Me" made the girls hysterical, while the title song, particularly as sung in the last frame, reduced them to tears.

Elvis' first movie, Love Me Tender *(1956), was not a rock-and-roll movie, but a Civil War drama shot in black and white. Elvis compensated for this by dynamically performing three country and western songs and turning a fourth, the title song, into one of his most popular hit singles.*

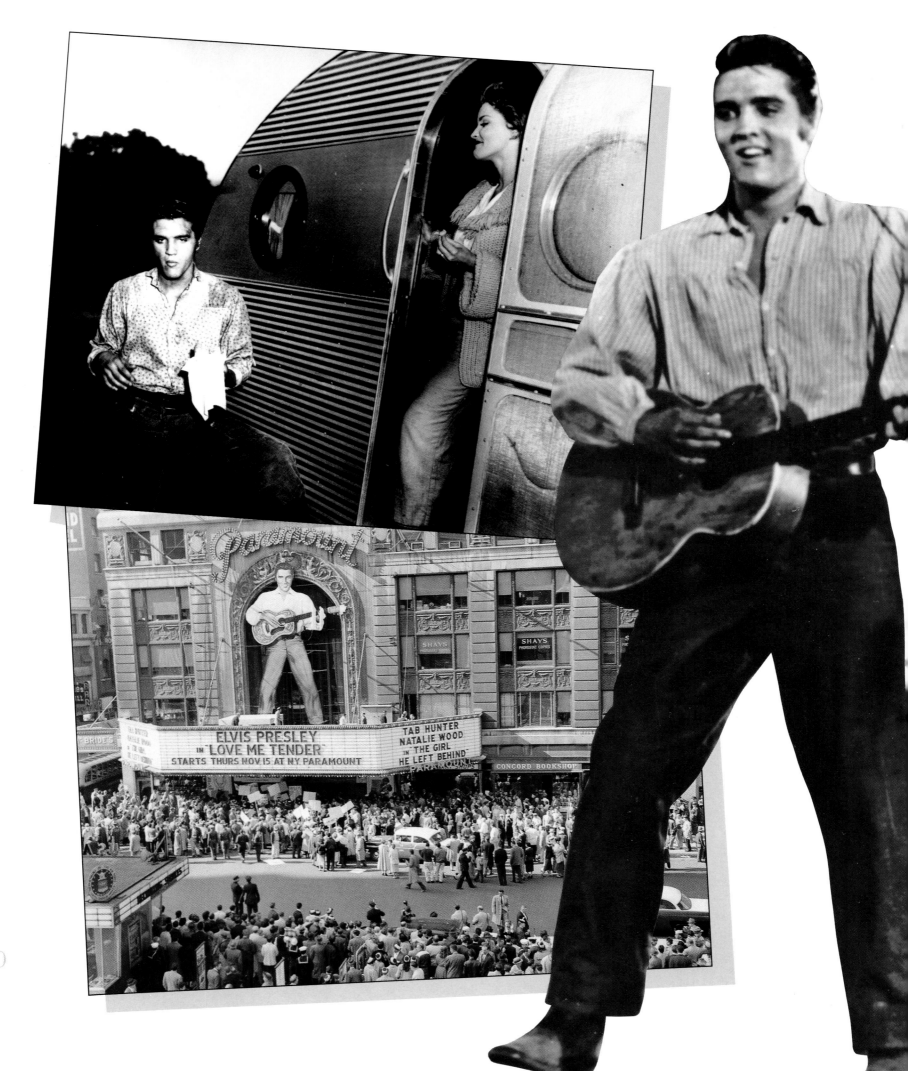

THE SONGS FOR *Love Me Tender* were recorded in August 1956 at Radio Recorders, 7000 Santa Monica Boulevard, Los Angeles. Also recorded there, but on September 6, was Elvis' great version of Leiber and Stoller's "Love Me," which was placed on the EP, *Elvis: Volume 1*. This EP actually reached the top of the singles charts, eventually selling over one million copies.

AS A FITTING TRIBUTE to his roots, Elvis ended the year by performing on December 22 at a benefit concert put on by Radio WDIA, the station that had exposed him to so much black rhythm and blues music. At the concert, Elvis performed with his heroes, B.B. King and "Mystery Train" composer and singer, Little Junior Parker.

Working conditions on Love Me Tender *(top left) were not glamorous, but the movie's New York opening certainly was, with an enormous cut-out of Elvis being unveiled to the delight of hundreds of fans (bottom left). From this black and white slice of Civil War corn, Elvis moved on to the full Technicolor glories of his second movie,* Loving You, *which had a plot that virtually duplicated his own rise to fame. It also had a great rock-and-roll soundtrack.*

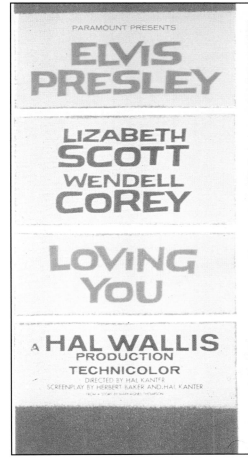

PARAMOUNT PRESENTS

ELVIS PRESLEY

LIZABETH SCOTT WENDELL COREY

LOVING YOU

A **HAL WALLIS** PRODUCTION **TECHNICOLOR**
DIRECTED BY HAL KANTER
SCREENPLAY BY HERBERT BAKER AND HAL KANTER

"WELL, MY DEARS, TUT-TUT AND BOSH-BOSH. JUDGING BY THE ANTI-ELVIS BELLOWS IN THE PARLORS, PRESS AND PUBS OF THOSE WHO WOULD BRAINWASH ANYBODY WHO DOESN'T MEET WITH THEIR APPROVAL, ELVIS IS A BIGGER MENACE TO THE U.S.A. THAN BULGANIN, KHRUSHCHEV AND OPIUM-SMOKING IN HIGH SCHOOL LUNCH ROOMS."
Fred Sparks, *Memphis Press-Scimitar*, January 7, 1957

TWO DAYS BEFORE HIS 19th birthday, on January 6, 1957, in a bid to win over the adults, Elvis sang his first sacred classic, "Peace in the Valley," on "The Sullivan Show." On January 13 he recorded it at Radio Recorders with the superb support of the Jordanaires. Even as he was doing so, his latest single, "Too Much," was becoming his eighth million-selling record. It was followed, in March, by his classic "All Shook Up," which also sold over a million, as well as adding a new phrase to the language.

HIS SECOND MOVIE, *Loving You*, went into production on January 21. Written specifically for him by Hal Kanter, who respected his talents, the screenplay is virtually the real-life Elvis Presley story with a little embroidery. It also takes a few digs at the machinations of managers, presumably like Colonel Parker, and the puritanism of those who were criticizing rock-and-roll in general and Elvis in particular. Though nothing wildly original, it has some biting dialogue, shows Elvis as he was onstage at that time – wild and sexy – and provides him with some real acting moments, none of which are missed. The movie is still a favorite with the fans.

THE SOUNDTRACK SONGS WERE recorded the same month, during production. While the title song (by Leiber and Stoller) is deceptively simple, its touching quality probably comes from the fact that Elvis insisted on over forty takes before he was satisfied. The ten-inch album contains a few classic rockers, notably "Party," "Mean Woman Blues," and "Gotta a Lotta Livin' to Do," but the biggest hit was "Teddy Bear," a whispering foot-tapper that convinced too many people that Elvis had a mania for stuffed teddy bears.

"IT WAS HIS FANS WHO DEFINED THE WORD 'DEVOTION' AND IT WAS ELVIS WHO WAS PROPAGATING THE FAITH. HE MAY NOT HAVE KNOWN WHAT HE HAD, BUT IT WAS CLEAR HE KNEW HE HAD IT."
Alfred Wertheimer, Photographer

THIS BELIEF BECAME SO widespread, particularly through the media, that for years after, Elvis was inundated with gifts of teddy bears from fans. This myth merely convinced more people that Elvis was an overgrown child, perhaps mentally retarded.

EARLY IN 1955 ELVIS celebrated his success by moving his family out of their old neighborhood and into a modest four-room house (now the Tiny Tot Nursery School) at 2414 Lamar Avenue. Six months later, in June, he moved them again,

this time into a grander, three-story house at 1414 Getwell Street. Finally, he bought his first house, located at 1034 Audubon Drive, in a wealthy, quiet area. The house cost what was then the huge sum of $40,000 and the Presleys moved in during March, 1956. Elvis also bought his mother a pink Cadillac which she had wanted, but she never got around to driving it.

LIFE IN AUDUBON DRIVE was not pleasant for Gladys. Dislocated from all she knew and watching Elvis being taken away from her by managers and fans alike, she was very unhappy. More problems came when the neighbors complained about the constant noise and activity caused by fans and the media. Eventually, the neighbors brought a public nuisance complaint against Elvis, and although the judge ruled in Elvis' favor, Gladys could only have been mortified to know that they weren't welcome in their new home.

When Elvis bought his twenty-three-room Memphis home, Graceland (left), in March 1957, he installed his beloved "music gates" and started collecting cars, including a pink Cadillac and a customized Cadillac of sprayed gold, with gold trim.

IN MARCH 1957, ELVIS purchased Graceland, a two-story, twenty-three-room mansion with thirteen acres of land, located at what is now 374 Elvis Presley Boulevard, Memphis. Soon after the purchase, he installed wrought-iron "music" gates and a swimming pool. He also raised the walls and planted trees for some privacy from the ever-present fans.

THOUGH MADE WITH THE best of intentions, the move to Graceland and an even more remote lifestyle only increased Gladys' secret drinking, hastening the deterioration in her health.

Jailhouse Rock (1957) produced the classic title song and the biggest controversy of Elvis' movie career. Public and critical opinion was divided between those who thought it a coarse exploitation flick and those who viewed it as an accurate satirical jab at the corruption of the pop music business. However, it presented Elvis with a meaty role and he gave one of his finest acting performances. As a "heavy" with a sharp edge of irony, he is completely convincing.

NOR WAS ELVIS TOO HAPPY. In an interview given to Joe Hyams of the New York *Herald Tribune,* he showed the hurt and confusion he was feeling over the barrage of criticisms levelled against him.

NEVERTHELESS, ON MAY 1, 1957, having completed his latest movie, he went into the MGM Studios in Culver city to make another. *Jailhouse Rock* is basically a repeat of *Loving You* – a poor boy makes good through his music – but in this case the poor boy is a hoodlum only redeemed in the last reel.

BECAUSE ELVIS PLAYS A thug and is given some biting lines ("That ain't tactics, honey, it's just the beast in me."), the movie is often discussed as one of his most realistic. In fact, the plot is ridiculous: Elvis goes to prison for manslaughter, is allowed, as a convict, to perform on a national TV show broadcast from the prison, becomes a star shortly after being released, treats everyone badly, and only realizes that all he needs is love when he almost loses his voice. In short, *Jailhouse Rock* is strictly a "B" movie only redeemed by some astringent dialogue and the handsomely mounted, superbly performed title song, which became an instant classic and huge hit single.

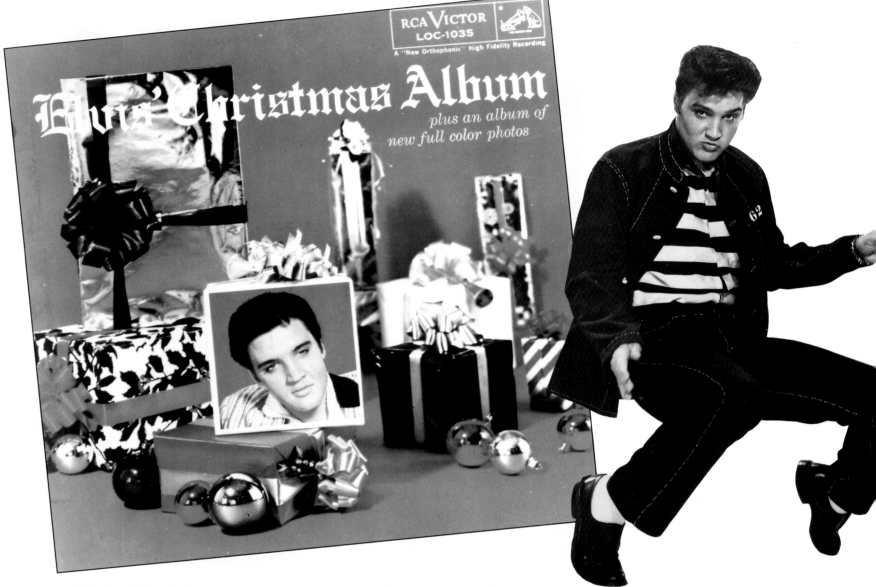

THE FACT THAT ELVIS gave an impressive performance in this movie was largely lost in the controversy that exploded over its general violence and cynicism, particularly the scene in which he is stripped to the waist and brutally flogged.

THE CRIES OF OUTRAGE were only increased with the release, in November, of *Elvis' Christmas Album*, which mixed some Christmas standards, including Bing Crosby's "White Christmas," with the sacred songs from Elvis' beautiful *Peace in the Valley* EP and some rock-and-roll Christmas songs, notably Leiber and Stoller's bluesy "Santa Claus is Back in Town." Elvis' superb, sexually suggestive performance of the latter, dropped casually into the middle of sacred songs and Christmas carols, led to nationwide accusations of "bad taste" and the banning of the album in certain quarters.

IRONICALLY, WITHIN DAYS, DURING Christmas week, advance orders for Elvis' new single "Don't" exceeded one million.

A SIMILAR REACTION WAS aroused by his next movie, *King Creole*, which began production in January 1958. Another film noir, but set in New Orleans, it features hoodlums, prostitutes, juvenile delinquents, and fights with broken

The now classic Elvis' Christmas Album, *with its extraordinary mix of hymns, seasonal classics and raunchy rock songs, caused as much controversy as the* Jailhouse Rock *movie and was even banned in some American states.*

Some fans were disappointed that Jailhouse Rock *was shot in grainy black and white and had only six songs on the soundtrack. Nevertheless, Elvis cut loose in the elaborate title-song sequence (bottom left), which he choreographed himself, turning it into one of his best.*

After serving time for manslaughter, the hard-as-nails Elvis of Jailhouse Rock *reads the fan mail (top left) he has received from women who saw him perform in a televised prison concert. The same violence that put him in prison drives him to smash his guitar when a foolish customer talks too loudly throughout his impromptu performance in a bar. The photo above is a posed shot based on the actual scene, which explains why Elvis is wearing his prison outfit.*

80

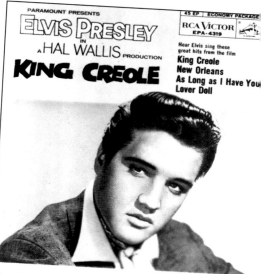

Elvis' last pre-army movie, King Creole (1958) was another violent melodrama set to music. Well written, superbly directed, and with a great supporting cast, it gained Elvis his best reviews yet and produced a terrific soundtrack album, more hit singles, and two chart-topping EPs.

bottles and flick knives. In this one, which many consider to be his best, Elvis once more plays a good boy forced into violence, but eventually redeemed through his music. Directed evocatively in black and white by Michael (*Casablanca*) Curtiz, with the strongest cast ever assembled around Elvis, *King Creole* is a knock-out combination of good drama and rock-and-roll, most of it jazz-and-blues-based. The film established Elvis as an actor of considerable promise. It also produced a soundtrack album that included some classic tracks, including "Hard Headed Woman," "Trouble," and the title song.

NEVERTHELESS, LIKE *JAILHOUSE ROCK*, *King Creole* was basically Hollywood's (or Colonel Parker's) clever way of pandering to the media's obsession with Elvis as a "white trash" singer, even as it was softening his image to make him acceptable to a wider, more conservative, audience.

AS ELVIS WAS ABOUT to be drafted into the army, their timing was perfect.

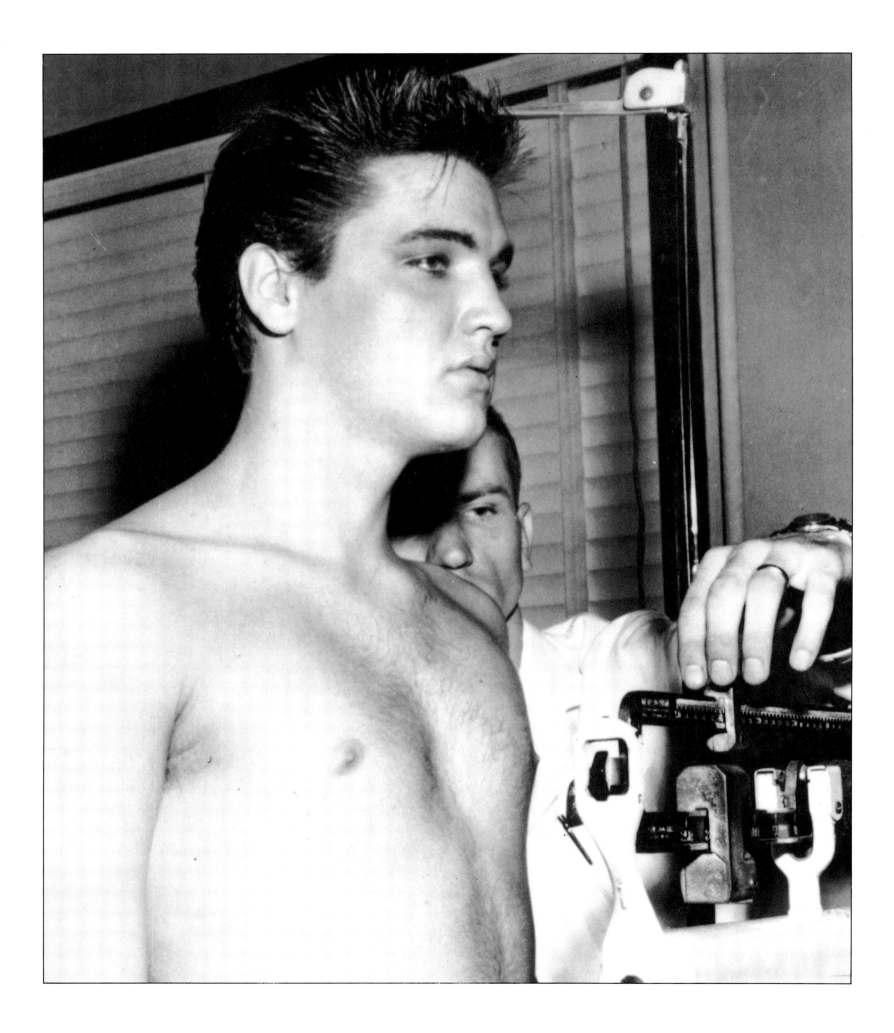

GI Blues

"I was in tanks for a long time, you see, and they rock and roll quite a bit."

Elvis Presley

O N DECEMBER 20, 1957, Milton Bowers, the Chairman of the Memphis Draft Board, announced that Uncle Sam wanted Elvis.

ON THE MONDAY MORNING of March 24, 1958, Elvis was inducted into the army at his local draft board on 198 South Main Street, Memphis, by Walter Alden (ironically the father of Ginger Alden, who would become Elvis' last girlfriend during the year of his death). Numerous friends saw Elvis off, including buddies Lamar Fike and Cliff Gleaves, girlfriend Anita Wood, and Elvis' parents. Vernon was anxious and Gladys was clearly ill.

ELVIS WAS GIVEN THE serial number, US53310761. After having his shots at Kennedy Hospital, he was shipped to Fort Chaffee Army Base, Arkanas, for indoctrination, physical examination, and aptitude tests. Then his beloved pompadour and sideburns were shaved off. This blasphemous act (for so did the fans view it) was witnessed by a horde of reporters and press photographers, as was every intimate moment of the whole procedure.

AT THE END OF MARCH, Elvis was shipped for eight weeks basic training to "A" Company, Second Medium Tank Battalion, Second Armored Division, at the army base at Fort Hood, Texas. Tiring of Colonel Parker's relentless media exposure of Elvis' every move, Lieutenant-Colonel Marjorie Shultern eventually had Parker ejected from the base.

WHILE STATIONED AT FORT HOOD, Elvis moved his folks into a small house in nearby Kileen. He also visited an old DJ friend, Eddie Fadal, who lived in Houston, Texas. Elvis, Fadal, and Anita Wood ate chili and sang a few songs, which Fadal recorded. Years later, in August 1977, Fadal released a bootleg record of the tapes on Memphis Flash Records. Called *Forever Young, Forever Beautiful*, the album contains their mutual singalong, some sung with records, some with Anita, and some with Elvis playing the piano.

Having been stripped to the waist to be flogged in Jailhouse Rock, *Elvis was stripped again, this time in full view of the media, to be inducted into the United States Army and become a respectable man. His fans were outraged.*

"NO. YOU GOT IT WRONG. I'M MISERABLE. I'M GUARDED. I CAN'T GO BUY MY OWN GROCERIES. I CAN'T GO TO THE MOVIES. I CAN'T SEE MY NEIGHBORS. I'M THE MOST MISERABLE WOMAN IN THE WORLD."
Gladys Presley

"A SURE WAY TO DEBASE YOUR MERCHANDISE IS TO GIVE IT AWAY."
Colonel Tom Parker, discussing Elvis

ANITA WOOD WAS ONE of Elvis' more highly publicized girlfriends of the time. A former DJ and Memphis TV personality, this vivacious, attractive blonde met Elvis in 1958 and dated him until his induction into the army. Rumors persisted that Elvis was going to marry her. In 1958 Anita recorded the Sun single, "I'll Wait Forever," but she waited in vain. The marriage never happened, though she and Elvis remained friends until the end.

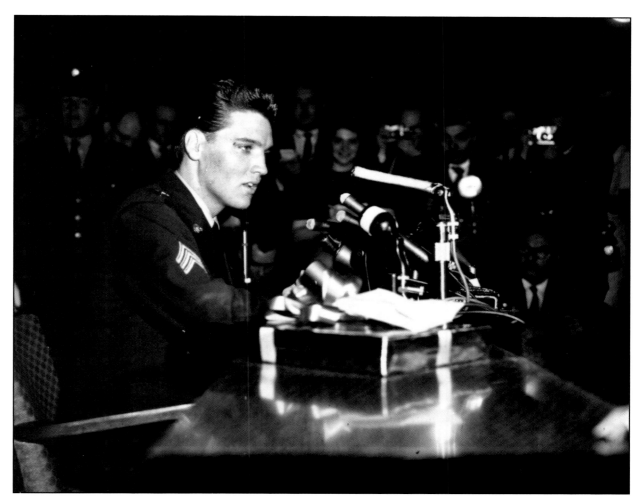

DURING HIS FOURTEEN-DAY furlough back in Memphis, starting on May 31, Elvis attended a preview of *King Creole* with his parents. He felt it was his best film and most of the critics agreed with him. Even the *New York Times*, formerly renowned for attacking Elvis, was forced to conclude: "The boy can act!" Meanwhile, his latest album, *Elvis' Golden Records*, and another single, "Wear my Ring Around your Neck," were racing up the album and singles charts respectively.

COLONEL PARKER ALSO ARRANGED for his "boy" to have another recording session at RCA Studios, Nashville. There, on June 10, with the aid of Chet Atkins, Floyd Cramer, D.J. Fontana, Hank Garland, the Jordanaires and other top musicians, Elvis produced five songs, four of which would scale the charts while he was still in the army. These were: "I Need your Love Tonight," "A Fool such as I," "I Got Stung" and "A Big Hunk o' Love." Then Elvis, just an ordinary soldier, returned to Fort Hood and his temporary home in nearby Kileen.

IN JULY, "HARD HEADED WOMAN," a song from *King Creole*, was a number one single. Two *King Creole* EPs were also high in the charts.

UNFORTUNATELY, IT WAS WHILE living in the small house in Kileen that an even more anxious, heavily-drinking Gladys Presley became seriously ill. Shocked by her appearance when he returned from basic training at Fort Hood, Elvis arranged for her to be taken back to Memphis and placed in intensive care in the Methodist Hospital. When it was announced that she was in a critical condition caused by acute hepatitis and severe liver damage, Elvis, who had been trying unsuccessfully to get emergency leave, threatened to go AWOL. Granted his request, he flew to his mother's side.

"OH, MY SON, MY SON!" Gladys was heard to cry out as they embraced.

ELVIS REMAINED WITH HER for twenty-four hours, then, at her insistence, he went to Graceland to get some sleep. In the early hours of Thursday, August 14, Vernon called to tell him that Gladys had died.

ELVIS WAS DEVASTATED. THE extraordinarily strong emotional ties between him and Gladys, which had been forged in both of them by the death of Jesse Garon, had made her the most important figure in his life. It was also common knowledge that when Elvis became rich and famous, his only real satisfaction was in being able to ease his mother's suffering. Unfortunately, he was only able to do this in a material way and, even as he was trying to better her life, he was removing her from the only world she knew and instilling in her the fear that she was losing him to managers, accountants, lawyers and, of course, his fans. Elvis had almost certainly sensed this, while not knowing how to deal with it, so the shock of losing her was bound to be compounded by the torment of guilt. Whatever his private thoughts, his feelings were soon evident to the whole world.

GLADYS WAS BURIED ON August 16, 1958, at the Forest Hill Cemetery, Memphis, located at what is now 1661 Elvis Presley Boulevard. The Blackwood Brothers sang two songs at her funeral: "Precious Memories" and "Rock of Ages." Elvis had to be dragged away from his mother's coffin, then he sobbed brokenly in his father's arms while photographers took pictures and microphones were shoved at him, turning his bereavement, grief and naked anguish into a public circus.

IF HE HAD NOT known the dark side of fame before, he was learning it now and would never forget it.

HE DRIED HIS TEARS in the privacy of Graceland, spending most of the nine days alone in his bedroom.

ON AUGUST 25, HE returned to Fort Hood, a man changed for all time.

ELVIS EMBARKED FOR GERMANY on the USS *General Randall*, leaving Military Ocean Terminal in Brooklyn, New York, on September 19, 1958, a month after his mother was buried. There, before the ship sailed, he held a press conference organized by Colonel Parker for later release on the all-talking EP, *Elvis Sails*.

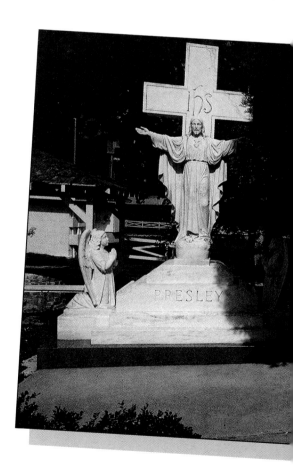

The early loss of Elvis' twin brother, Jesse Garon, combined with Vernon Presley's many absences, had made the relationship between Elvis and his mother much closer than normal. Also, Elvis and his mother had attended the Pentecostal churches of Tupelo and believed implicitly in the hereafter. When Gladys passed away, Elvis must have assumed that she had gone to join Jesse Garon, but when she died, something also died inside Elvis. The magical inner light he had possessed was dimmed overnight.

AS IT HAD BEEN with Gladys' funeral, so it was with Elvis' departure for Germany. Present, apart from the horde of reporters, photographers, fans and a military brass band playing Elvis Presley tunes, were Colonel Parker, Jean and Julian Aberbach and Freddie Bienstock from Hill and Range Songs, and the whole gang from RCA Records. Looking drawn, but stunningly handsome in his uniform, Elvis answered the queries of the press with grace and good humor.

WHEN HE DISEMBARKED AT Bremerhaven on October 1, he was greeted by hundreds of screaming German fans and the same media circus.

POSTED TO FRIEDBERG, NOT far from Frankfurt, he rented a house at 14 Goethestrasse, in Bad Nauheim, and moved in with Vernon, Minnie Mae, Red West and Lamar Fike. When not performing his duties as a tank driver, he dated an attractive seventeen-year-old, blonde German, Margit Buergin. This ambitious

In the September following his induction into the army on March 24, 1958, Elvis embarked for Germany on the USS General Randall. *During his service Elvis was by no means forgotten, with Colonel Parker organizing press conferences, RCA repackaging various compillation sets and his first four movies being re-released. Magazines were full of speculation about Elvis' current romances and* Elvis Monthly, *the first fan magazine was produced.*

Silver Screen

Elvis Presley: Will he comeback—or fizzle?

APRIL · 25¢

arol Lynley: ho says e's lonely?

ilah Graham's ate Gossip!

Perkins: of bliss"

ELVIS PRESLEY

PHOTOPLAY

★

MARCH 25¢

why Liz had to leave the party so early

CONTEST win a "welcome home" DATE WITH ELVIS

(see page 19)

CAROL LYNLEY:

honest, you can dress like a movie star, too

"HE ENDS ON A FULL-VOICED CADENCE, A-G-F, THAT HAS NOTHING TO DO WITH THE VOCAL DEVICES OF RHYTHM-AND-BLUES OR COUNTRY. THAT A IS HIT RIGHT ON THE NOSE …. ELVIS IS, IN A WORD, AN EXTRAORDINARY VOICE – OR MANY VOICES."
Henry Pleasants, *The Great American Popular Singers*

young lady, who wanted to be a model or movie actress, soon found herself in the middle of a publicity whirlwind, with pictures of her and Elvis, or of her posing alone, being distributed worldwide by the press. She returned to instant oblivion when Elvis stopped seeing her.

OTHER, LESS PUBLICIZED DATES in Germany were the eighteen-year-old Elisabeth Stefaniak, who became his secretary and translator in Bad Nauheim, and Vera Tchechowa, a dark, sensual Russian-born movie actress.

SHORTLY AFTER MARGIT'S DEPARTURE, Currie Grant, an officer with the Army Special Services, introduced Elvis to Priscilla Beaulieu at a party in Elvis' house on Goethestrasse. Priscilla was the exceptionally beautiful, dark-haired, adopted daughter of Air Force Major Joseph P. Beaulieu, then stationed in Wiesbaden. Though the lovely Priscilla was then only fourteen, Major Beaulieu gave

91

permission for Elvis to date her, provided they be chaperoned. Elvis agreed. But the chaperons did not stop the media from speculating feverishly about him and his fourteen-year-old beauty.

ACCORDING TO PRISCILLA, THOUGH she and Elvis were in love, they did not consummate their love in Germany and Elvis continued bedding other women.

ROMANCE WAS ALSO BLOSSOMING elsewhere. While Elvis was seeing Priscilla, his father began dating Mrs. Davada "Dee" Elliot Stanley, the petite, blonde, blue-eyed wife of Bill Stanley, a non-commissioned officer stationed at Elvis' base in Freidberg. Coming so soon after the death of his mother, Elvis was deeply shocked by this affair but said nothing to his father or Dee. Though he often complained

"[ELVIS] OBLITERATED DISTINCTIONS BETWEEN MUSICAL FORMS …. MANY SINGERS OF OUR ERA MIGHT HAVE RECORDED BITS OF DEVILTRY LIKE 'ONE NIGHT' AND 'ALL SHOOK UP.' NO ONE ELSE COULD ALSO HAVE MADE A HYMN LIKE 'CRYING IN THE CHAPEL' A CONVINCING HIT. IT WOULD HAVE OCCURRED TO NO ONE ELSE TO TRY TO SPAN THE GULF BETWEEN THOSE SONGS."
Dave Marsh, writer

bitterly to Priscilla about the affair, when his father and Dee asked for his "permission" to marry, he swallowed his bile and said, "Yes." He swallowed even more bile when Vernon later said he was going to move Dee and her two sons into Graceland, the home Elvis now viewed as a shrine to his mother. Elvis would never fully forgive his father for doing this.

WHILE STATIONED AT FRIEDBERG, he formed close friendships with two army buddies, Joe Esposito and Charlie Hodge. Both would spend a lot of time with him at 14 Goethestrasse and later, back in Graceland, become members of his so-called Memphis Mafia.

BORED MINDLESS BY THE army, Elvis began practising karate in the house on Goethestrasse. He also started taking Dexedrine to keep him awake during army maneuvers. This soon became as regular a habit as his karate, eventually leading to his full-blown drug dependence.

DURING A VISIT TO the Moulin Rouge, a Munich nightclub, he was photographed by Rudolf Paulini. The photographs of a mostly dead-eyed, emotionally frozen Elvis embracing or kissing waitresses, showgirls, fans, and prostitutes, later found their way into the hands of filmmaker Diego Cortez, who reproduced them in a book, *Private Elvis* (1978). This seedily fascinating item was described neatly by writer Griel Marcus as a "pornographic" picture of "American health in a smashup with European decay."

WHILE THE SUPPOSEDLY "PRIVATE" Private Elvis was visiting nightclubs, bedding German women, falling in love with the fourteen-year-old Priscilla Beaulieu, and taking part in maneuvers with the 32nd Tank Battalion, his star was not dimming in the West. The all-talking *Elvis Sails* EP was selling briskly; "A Fool such as I" and its flipside, "I Need your Love Tonight," was becoming his nineteenth consecutive million-selling record; "A Big Hunk o' Love" was about to race up the charts; and two albums of mostly old tracks, For *LP Fans Only* and *A Date with Elvis,* were very successful.

EVEN WHILE ELVIS WAS still on maneuvers near Frankfurt, producer Hal Wallis was in the same area, shooting background scenes for Elvis' first post-army movie, naturally about a GI who could sing really well and appropriately entitled *GI Blues.* Learning this, Elvis became even more depressed.

TO COVER THE BARREN Christmas before Elvis' demob, RCA repackaged his controversial *Elvis' Christmas Album* from the previous year and released it with two more compilation sets: *50,000,000 Elvis Fans Can't be Wrong* and *Elvis' Gold Records – Volume 2*. All were hot sellers.

MEANWHILE, NUMEROUS "TRIBUTE" RECORDS about him were being released; a book about his army career, *Operation Elvis*, was going into production; his first four movies were re-released to great business; and Albert Hand produced the first editions of *Elvis Monthly*, a fan magazine that was distributed worldwide by the British Elvis Presley Fan Club.

IN JANUARY, 1960, PRIVATE ELVIS was promoted to sergeant and placed in command of a three-man reconnaissance team for the Third Armored Division's 32nd Scout Platoon. He performed his duties admirably, was photographed and filmed constantly while doing so, and became the darling of the conservative, middle-aged parents who had previously despised him.

BY MARCH, WHEN ELVIS was due to be demobbed, the career of Jerry Lee Lewis was in shreds, Little Richard had gone into a seminary, Buddy Holly, Ritchie Valens and the Big Bopper were dead, Gene Vincent was already on the road to ruin, and Elvis' only real competitors were Ricky Nelson, Frankie Avalon, Bobby Darin, and Elvis lookalike, Fabian.

ON MARCH 3, 1960, after a monstrous press conference staged by the army, a greatly changed Elvis returned to America and a whole new career.

Private Elvis became Sergeant Elvis, finished his two-year stint, and returned to America in the middle of a snowstorm. By this time many were wondering if he could regain his title after such a long time out of the ring. They were soon to find out ....

95

The Hollywood Years

"He had created his own world.
He had to. There was
nothing else for him to do."

Johnny Rivers

ELVIS RETURNED HOME ON March 3, 1960, landing in a blizzard on McGuire Air Force Base, opposite Fort Dix in northern New Jersey. Shortly after his return, Tennessee senator Estes Kefauver inserted a tribute to him in the Congressional Record.

The Elvis who returned to America in March 1960 was more of a matinée idol than a greasy rocker. He was also changed in other, more disturbing ways, though this was hidden behind his unique, lopsided grin.

ELVIS LET HIS HAIR grow longer, but now kept his sideburns shaved and looked for all the world like a regular guy. While he was as charming and good-humored as ever in interviews, those who shared his life in Graceland could see that he was not the same person.

THOUGH STILL THOUGHTFUL AND generous, he was now prone to outbursts of temper. He also spent too much time alone in his bedroom, sometimes just staring at the walls. Occasionally he would be overheard "talking" to his dead mother or to Jesse Garon.

LUCKILY, HE WAS SOON back at work.

THOUGH ONE OF HIS singing idols, Frank Sinatra, had described rock-and-roll as "played and written by goons for the most part for goons," disastrous ratings for his own TV shows forced him to eat crow by inviting the new, slick Elvis to appear on his "Timex Special" broadcast of March 26, 1960. Disguised as a welcome home for Elvis, this attempt to boost Sinatra's falling ratings was broadcast from the Fontainbleau Hotel in Miami. It was notable for the fact that Elvis, still shorn of his sideburns, was wearing a black tux with bow tie, just like Sinatra.

AFTER PERFORMING BOTH SIDES of his new single, "Stuck on You" and "Fame and Fortune," Elvis duetted with Sinatra on "Love Me Tender," then performed Sinatra's golden oldie, "Witchcraft." Though Elvis looked uncomfortable, the show

Many fans were shocked when the post-army Elvis appeared on television with the arch-enemy of rock-and-roll, Frank Sinatra (left). While giving Sinatra's slipping ratings an enormous boost, the appearance did little for Elvis, other than proving that he could look as smooth, and sing as smoothly, as the best of them. In fact, this was a deliberate sign of intent.

The title of Elvis' first post-army album, Elvis is Back, *was another firm sign of intent. Though perhaps looking too smooth on the front cover, and while shamelessly exploiting his army service with the back and inner sleeve photos, Elvis certainly proved with this classic work that he had lost none of his extraordinary vocal talent. Blues, ballads, country weepers, "doo-wop," and rockers were intermingled with stunning aplomb. The competition was wiped out overnight.*

"I WAS DOUBLED OVER, GRIPPING MY STOMACH WITH AN ATTACK OF NERVES. SUDDENLY, THERE HE WAS BENDING OVER ME ASKING, 'IS THERE ANYTHING WRONG, MA'AM?' I SAID I WAS GOING TO MAKE A SCREEN TEST AND COULDN'T GET MY STOMACH TO STOP CHURNING. AND IF I WASN'T SURPRISED ENOUGH ALREADY, HE SAID, 'I FEEL THAT WAY EVERY DAY OF MY LIFE, MA'AM.' "
Maureen Stapleton, actress

was a great success, which certainly boosted Sinatra's ratings and did Elvis no harm.

THE *ELVIS IS BACK* album came out of his first two post-army recording sessions at RCA Nashville Studio, one on March 20, another on April 3. Its first track was a flashy, full-bodied production of Otis Blackwell's rhythm and blues rocker, "Make Me Know it." Stereo was then in its infancy, and the sweeping, Phil Spectorish sound on this number, as heard in stereo, made for a dazzling opener. It was followed immediately, cleverly, with a bare-as-bones, sizzling rendition of "Fever" and an immaculate "teen" foot-tapper, "The Girl of my Best Friend." "Fame and Fortune" was a superbly rendered lament about the worthlessness of fame without love, "Thrills of your Love" was an erotically charged ballad, "I Will be Home Again" was beautifully sung country corn, and "Such a Night" and "Dirty, Dirty Feelings" were all-out, sexually suggestive rockers. However, what made the album truly outstanding was the inclusion of three blues songs, notably the classic "Reconsider Baby," with Elvis' rhythm guitar giving impetus to a band that was as hot as they come. It included his old pals Scotty Moore, J.D. Fontana, Floyd Cramer, and the Jordanaires, as well as the legendary Boots Randolph on saxophone.

99

ELVIS IS BACK CONFIRMED his mastery of every pop idiom and instantly laid waste to the competition. His first post-army single, "Stuck on You," was viewed delightedly by many fans as a deliberate statement of intent. Another single was "It's Now or Never," an updated version of "O Sol Mio", which Elvis sings under the influence of Mario Lanza and Enrico Caruso, his operatic idols.

THE SINGLE SHOCKED MILLIONS because it was clearly not rock-and-roll. It also thrilled millions because Elvis sang it beautifully to an immaculate backing, noted for the unforgettable melodic counterpoint played by pianist Floyd Cramer. "It's Now or Never" became one of the biggest single successes in pop history, selling over nine million copies. It was followed quickly by another, slower ballad, "Are You Lonesome Tonight?", an old Al Jolson weepie that had also been a hit for the Ink Spots. Elvis and the Jordanaires simply imitated the Ink Spots, but added the novelty of a soulful spoken bridge. Saleswise, the single was another monster, selling over five million. It also indicated in which direction Elvis was heading – well away from rock-and-roll.

The exploitation of Elvis' army service continued with his first post-army movie, GI Blues. This did not please Elvis, though he performed with great charm in what turned out to be a well crafted romantic comedy. He then returned to a different kind of fun and games in Graceland, surrounded by his Memphis Mafia and other acolytes.

ANY DOUBTS ABOUT THAT were firmly laid to rest with the release of his first post-army film. *GI Blues* (1960) is an exploitation movie that cashed in on Elvis' two years in the army. It is the story of a GI who can sing up a storm and is serving his country with a tank battalion based near Frankfurt. Any resemblance to persons living is purely intentional, but this particular Private Elvis hardly gets near rock-and-roll and instead sings pretty ballads, some old German folk songs, some military pop numbers, and even a lullaby. He is no longer backed by rock

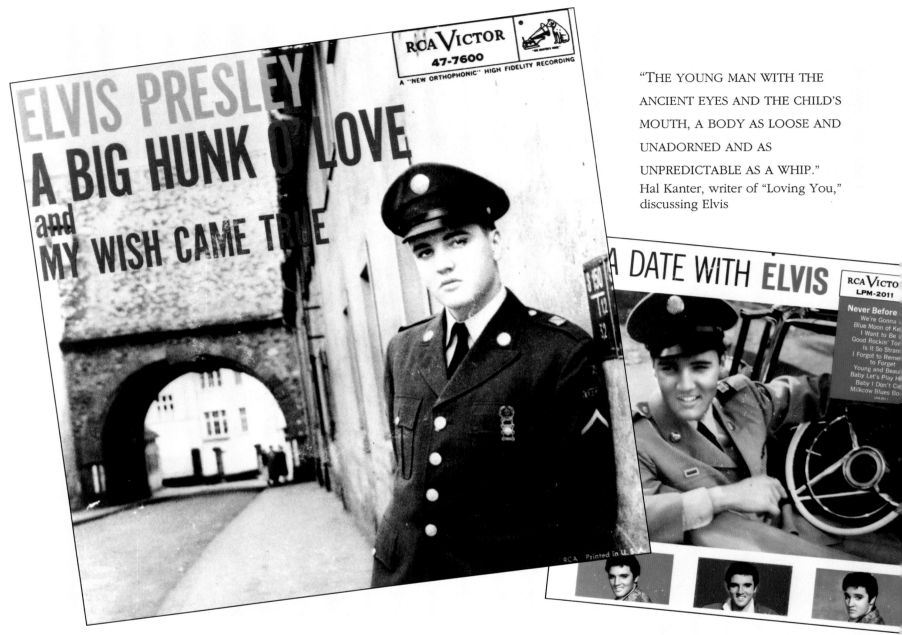

musicians, but by actors pretending to be musicians, and he doesn't sing in juke-joints or smoky nightclubs, but in beer gardens, cable cars, trains and baby's bedrooms, to children, puppets, the army and, of course, babies.

THOUGH *GI BLUES* SHOCKED many rock-and-roll fans, it was expertly made, co-starred the dynamic Juliet Prowse, and became a huge hit at the box office.

IN APRIL, 1960, ELVIS rented 565 Perugia Way, an Oriental-styled mansion with gardens and swimming pool, adjacent to the Bel Air Golf Club. After moving in with his buddies, he had the garden ripped out and replaced with a recreation room, including pool tables, a jukebox, and cinema for home screenings. It was in Perugia Way that he first started displaying an unhealthy egomania that had not been seen before. This first took the form of deliberately late entrances to his private movie screenings for friends. He would emerge dramatically from between sliding panels, often in elaborate costumes: the "staged" entrance of an old-fashioned Hollywood star.

The promise shown with Elvis' first post-army album, Elvis is Back, *was not followed through. While he had many of his biggest selling singles during this period, including the astoundingly successful "It's Now or Never," he was already slipping towards a routine of uninspiring compilation albums, movie soundtracks, and correspondingly bland studio portraits.*

ON APRIL 26, PRODUCTION began on *GI Blues*. Elvis expressed his distaste for the production to his buddies, but said nothing to those in charge. The songs, he informed Priscilla Beaulieu, "aren't worth a cat's ass." He may have been consoled by what the press were convinced was his intense and intimate relationship with the fiery Juliet Prowse, who had just emerged unscathed from a similar relationship with Frank Sinatra. To complicate matters, the press was also filled with assertions that Elvis and Sinatra's daughter, the delectable Nancy, were also romantically involved.

ON JULY 3, 1960, Vernon married the former Davada "Dee" Elliot Stanley and moved her into Graceland with her three small sons, Billy, Rick, and David. Elvis resented this enough to rip down the curtains that Dee put up in his absence, then he made Vernon move out with Dee, though he soon relented and invited them back, putting them into a separate building near the mansion. Thereafter he treated Dee with cautious respect and was particularly generous to her three boys.

THOUGH DEE WOULD CONTINUE to have problems living in Graceland, most were not caused by Elvis, but by her always tumultuous relationship with Vernon.

ELVIS WAS WELL OUT of it. On August 8, 1960, production began on Don Siegel's *Flaming Star*. As the role had originally been conceived for Marlon

A mystery composite photo (above). The nature of the various superimpositions suggests that Colonel Parker (with the hat) is giving out promotional GI Blues albums to the production crew of Flaming Star. *Left: Elvis with co-star Barbara Eden.*

Brando, one of Elvis' two favorite actors (James Dean was the other), he was naturally excited by the prospect of working in it. He would not be disappointed. Skillfully directed by Siegel, Elvis' portrayal of an Indian halfbreed divided in his loyalties would be totally convincing and the movie itself would be a minor gem.

UNFORTUNATELY, SINCE IT HAD only a brief snatch of song at the beginning, as well as the title song sung over the credits, *Flaming Star* was only moderately successful at the box office. While it did not lose money, it was measured against *GI Blues* and found wanting. Any hopes Elvis had about being a serious actor were dashed with the release of his next movie, *Wild in the Country*, which went into production on November 7, 1960, virtually straight after *Flaming Star*. Produced by the esteemed Jerry Wald, written by the acclaimed playwright Clifford Odets, directed by the award-winning Philip Dunne, and with a rock-solid cast including Hope Lange, Millie Perkins, John Ireland, and the "cult" actress, Tuesday Weld, *Wild in the Country* was a prestigious production that just didn't work. Elvis again showed that he had strong acting potential, but the lackluster script and relative absence of songs caused it to fare no better than *Flaming Star*.

106

With two movies produced in 1960, Elvis again attempted to gain recognition as a serious actor. In Flaming Star *(right), he gave a convincing portrayal of a half-breed Indian forced to take sides. In* Wild in the Country, *with Tuesday Weld (above), his performance veered with the uncertain script, though he still managed well in the better scenes.*

With the relative box-office failure of Elvis' two "serious" movies, the die was cast for a string of unadventurous forays into safe musical travelogues. The Elvis starring in them was still exceptionally handsome, but seemed increasingly unreal.

"HE SAID, 'WHERE ARE YOU GOING?' I SAID, 'I'M GOING TO ORLANDO.' HE SAID, 'MAN, THAT'S THE WRONG DIRECTION. BUT THEN, YOU WERE ALWAYS GOING THE WRONG WAY, WEREN'T YOU?' WE ALL LAUGHED, AND I SAID, 'WELL, ELVIS, THAT ALL DEPENDS ON WHERE YOU'RE COMING FROM.' "
Pat Boone

THE DIE WAS BEING cast for Elvis' dismal future in lightweight musical comedies.

IN THE MEANTIME, HE was still succeeding on other levels. His first sacred album, *His Hand in Mine*, was beautifully sung and critically acclaimed. *Billboard* magazine named "It's Now or Never" the vocal single of the year. The National Academy of Recording Arts and Sciences awarded him five Grammy nominations, three for "Are You Lonesome Tonight?" and two for *GI Blues*. On March 8, 1961, he appeared by special invitation before the General Assembly of the Legislature of Tennessee, where Buford Ellington, the Governor of Tennessee, made him an honorary Colonel, just like "Colonel" Tom Parker. "Surrender," another rehashed operatic song, albeit sung superbly, was followed by a genuine rock single, the pounding "Little Sister" backed by the even more popular "Marie's the Name of His Latest Flame." He had different hit singles simultaneously in England, Germany and the United States, with more gold records rolling in his direction.

WITH THE DISAPPOINTMENT OF the "serious" movies still to come, he was able, at least for the time being, to bury his private grief in creative success.

STILL IN LOVE WITH Priscilla, Elvis invited her to stay at Graceland for Christmas. The following year he asked Major Beaulieu if she could move to Graceland for good. It is a tribute to Elvis' legendary charm that the otherwise level-headed major agreed, on the condition that Elvis promised, in effect, to become her legal guardian, enroling her in school, and providing his father and stepmother as legal guardians. Elvis agreed, and Priscilla moved into Graceland to begin an unusual, still enigmatic, relationship.

FROM 1962 TO 1968, from when she was fifteen to twenty-one, Priscilla was "raised" by Elvis in Graceland. Their relationship was odd, to say the least. Priscilla was a natural beauty who required little make-up, but Elvis made her wear the clothes, heavy make-up, and grotesque hair-styles of a Las Vegas showgirl. Though they often shared the same bed and played childish sexual games, they did not properly consummate their relationship until they were married five years later.

MIXED UP IN ALL this was Elvis' old-fashioned, puritanical notion of "respecting" his future wife and having a "virgin" bride, even though he was bedding an endless stream of other women. However, there is also the undeniable fact that the young Priscilla bore a striking resemblance to Elvis; even more so when her auburn hair was dyed black at his request. As Elvis had dyed his own brownish hair black (to make him look more like his mother, according to some), it is possible that his attempts to change Priscilla's appearance related to fantasies about getting back the "psychic soulmate" he had lost through the death of Jesse Garon.

WHATEVER THE REASON, NONE of it sat easily with Priscilla. Even worse was the fact that Elvis was absent more often than not, either making movies on location or sleeping most of the day, emerging at night only to idle the time away

109

with his buddies and the girls they brought in for him. For this reason Priscilla soon became disenchanted, as well as increasingly lonesome.

STILL, IT WAS A life like no other, so she just hung in there, observing the rise and fall of her husband, one of the world's most famous men.

ON FEBRUARY 25, 1961, Elvis gave two shows at the Ellis Auditorium in Memphis, in aid of local charities and his own Under-Privileged Children's project in Tupelo. Playing with him were Scotty Moore, J.D. Fontana, Floyd Cramer, Boots Randolph, and the Jordanaires. Wearing a white dinner jacket, black trousers and

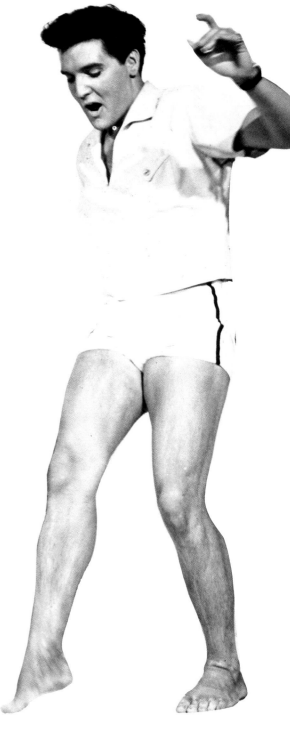

tie, Elvis sang seventeen songs, including his latest hit, "Surrender." He climaxed with a scream-inducing rendition of "Hound Dog." A month later, on March 25, he gave a show in the Bloch Arena, Pearl Harbor, Hawaii, to benefit the USS *Arizona* Memorial Fund. This time, he wore a gold lamé jacket and sang nineteen songs, making it his longest show ever.

THAT WAS THE LAST live appearance Elvis would make for eight years.

HOWEVER, THE LACK OF touring did not help Priscilla, as Colonel Parker replaced it with a relentless schedule of movies, most of which were shot on

In March 1961 Elvis gave his final live performance for almost nine years in the Bloch Arena, Pearl Harbor, Hawaii. A month later, he returned to make the first of his "beach and bikini" movies, Blue Hawaii.

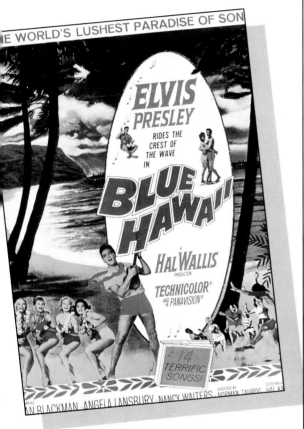

While Blue Hawaii *was regarded by many to be yet another sign of a sell-out by the former King of rock-and-roll, it was phenomenally successful at the box office and the soundtrack became Elvis' biggest grossing album to date.*

location. Soon, Elvis would be making an average of four movies per year, which meant he was rarely at home.

SHORTLY AFTER THE HAWAIIAN concert, perhaps knowing he was embarked on a long career in movies, he moved from Perugia Way into a baronial mansion with an enormous marble entrance hall and basement bowling alley, located at 1059 Bellagio Road in Bel Air. Finding it too big and eerie, he soon moved back to the house on Perugia Way.

ON APRIL 3, 1961, he returned to Hawaii to begin work on his next movie, *Blue Hawaii.* During shooting, he developed a genuine love of the islands and a

"HEY, THERE WERE SOME PRETTY FUNNY THINGS IN THIS SCRIPT. I'M GOING TO HAVE TO READ IT SOME DAY."
Elvis, shooting a movie

growing fascination with Hawaiian mythology and Polynesian culture. He began calling Colonel Parker "Kuhuna," after the Hawaiian gods of that name, and it is probable that his later obsession with all kinds of mysticism and religious philosophy took root in the islands.

BLUE HAWAII CAN JUSTIFIABLY be called the first of Elvis' "beach and bikini" movies. A competent romantic comedy with lovely scenery, attractive girls, and fourteen songs, mostly quasi-Hawaiian ballads (including his classic, "Can't Help Falling in Love"), it made a fortune at the box-office and its soundtrack alone sold

113

over six million dollars worth of LPs. Following hot on the heels of Elvis' two commercial failures, *Flaming Star* and *Wild in the Country*, it became the biggest film of his career.

ELVIS WENT STRAIGHT FROM the song-packed *Blue Hawaii* into two movies with few songs and slightly more ambitious plots. The first, which began production on July 3, 1961, was *Follow That Dream*. Though displaying a considerable talent for comedy in this film, Elvis also played the first of the roles written by those in Hollywood who viewed him as a stereotyped southern halfwit. This was followed in October by the remake of the 1937 boxing movie, *Kid Galahad*, which attempted to mix drama with music and failed on both counts.

FROM THIS POINT ON, Elvis was doomed to a whole string of movies based on the successful *Blue Hawaii*: scenic locations, beautiful girls, cute children and animals, sports cars, motor boats, airplanes, and plenty of songs.

ELVIS WOULD SOON COME to loathe making the movies, but his fans would take longer to start staying away.

IN ALL FAIRNESS, SOME of them weren't all that bad. In March, 1962, production began on *Girls! Girls! Girls!* which was almost as good as, or no worse than, *Blue Hawaii*. It was greatly aided by the wonderful Stella Stevens and a soundtrack that included the hit single, "Return to Sender." Also, in July 1963, production began on what was undoubtedly the best of the post-army movie musicals: *Viva Las Vegas*, co-starring the terrific Ann-Margret.

IRONICALLY, ANN-MARGRET HAD found fame in *Bye Bye Birdie* (1963), a movie adapted from the 1962 Broadway musical about the induction of a rock-and-roll singer into the army – clearly based on Elvis. Ann-Margret's frantic, sensual dancing in that film was repeated without delay in *Viva Las Vegas* (1963), but she was even more electrifying when teamed with Elvis in the "C'mon Everybody" rock number.

Though Elvis movies were becoming increasingly bland, they were not yet complete disasters. Girls! Girls! Girls! (1962) wasn't much brighter than its title, but at least it had some decent tunes, including the title song and the classic "Return to Sender." It also had cute Laurel Goodwin (above left) and the always excellent Stella Stevens. It was followed by the last good Elvis movie, Viva Las Vegas (1963), in which he co-starred with the electrifying Ann-Margret (right). As the sparks flew between them, both on and off the set, they managed to set fire to the box office. The movie became Elvis' biggest grosser since Blue Hawaii.

IT WAS AN OPEN secret that Elvis and Ann-Margret were a serious item at the time – even Priscilla knew about it. This·may explain why Ann-Margret was allowed to perform with Elvis and why he played so well against her. *Viva Las Vegas* has some real rock-and-roll, a couple of well staged dances, a rocking Elvis Presley, and a witty, sexy, singing co-star. Unfortunately, it was the last good Elvis musical.

By now each Elvis movie was merging seamlessly into the other and the viewer could scarcely tell the difference between them. In a sense, 1961's Blue Hawaii *(top left), 1962's* It Happened at the World's Fair *(right), and 1965's* Frankie and Johnny *(below), were all basically the same colorful, unimpressive movie ...*

... and when they ran short of bikinis and sports cars, as they did in 1963's Kissin' Cousins *(left), they just wheeled on a cute kid or big animal!*

MIKE EDWARDS

OTHER MOVIES OF THIS period were *It Happened at the World's Fair* (1962), *Fun in Acapulco* (1963), and the two Sam "King of the Quickies" Katzman productions, *Kissin' Cousins* (1963) and *Harum Scarum* (1965). The first has Elvis nonsensically involved with an incredibly "cute" child. In the second, he sings Mexican ballads to Ursula Andress, but redeems himself by diving off a cliff into the ocean and, more importantly, by performing "Bossa Nova Baby." The third is a re-run of his country-rube image (with the added novelty of having him playing twins, one dark-haired, one fair); and the fourth has him togged up in Arabian robes and turban, like Rudolph Valentino. *Tickle Me* (1964) was produced so cheaply, the producers even used old Elvis songs; and after *Paradise, Hawaiian Style* (1966), a poor remake of *Blue Hawaii*, it was almost impossible to imagine that his movies could become even worse ... but somehow they did.

IN 1965 ELVIS MOVED into a modern house at 10050 Rocca Place, situated in

117

Stone Canyon near the Bel Air Hotel. There he continued his increasingly isolated life with his so-called Memphis Mafia and their girlfriends or wives.

THE MEMPHIS MAFIA – ALSO known as "El's Angels" and the TCB (Taking Care of Business) group – were all friends from Elvis' earlier days, now gathered around him either to run his day-to-day business or simply to keep him entertained. Joe Esposito, whom Elvis had first met in the army in Germany, was his bookkeeper, the foreman of his roadshow, and his personal aide and most trusted friend. Charlie Hodge, whom Elvis also met in the army, played rhythm guitar on Elvis' albums, sometimes sang vocal harmonies, and was a general gofer in Graceland. Lamar Fike, an Elvis fan during the early days who became a trusted employee, worked on Elvis' behalf at Hill and Range Songs and was known for his ballooning weight and good humor. (A trusted friend who increasingly took the brunt of Elvis' mockery, he later got his own back by collaborating with Albert Goldman on the notorious biography *Elvis*.) Marty Lacker was Elvis' personal secretary, bookkeeper, and confidanté. Jerry Schilling, bodyguard and one of Elvis' closest friends, was also a talented, articulate administrator. Billy Smith, Elvis' favorite cousin, was his valet and personal assistant. Also in the Memphis Mafia were his other bodyguards: David Hebler and the brothers Red and Sonny West.

IN 1965, ELVIS' ONLY contact with the rapidly changing music scene was when he had occasional visits from other singers or groups, such as the Beatles, who came to see him that August. By then, when Elvis was recording dross like "Rock a Hula Baby" and "There's No Room to Rhumba in a Sports Car," the Beatles had five consecutive number one hits and Elvis was beginning to seem like a lost cause.

THERE ARE VARYING REPORTS about his meeting with the Beatles, some saying that they jammed enthusiastically all afternoon, others saying that conversation was strained. What is not in doubt is that by 1965 Elvis was virtually divorced from rock-and-roll, not too happy about it, and living the life of a pampered, bored celebrity in Bel Air and Memphis.

WHEN HOME IN GRACELAND, Elvis practised karate, went horse riding with Priscilla on his private ranch, watched too much television, fooled around with loaded pistols, and played football with show business friends and the Memphis Mafia. (He named his football team "Elvis Presley Enterprises" after the company formed in 1954 by his first manager, Bob Neal.) He threw many late-night parties at the popular Memphis restaurant, Chanault's, located at 1402 Bellevue Boulevard. He regularly rented the Crosstown Theater, the Memphian Theater, or the Avon Theater at 124 West Broadway, West Memphis, for all-night movie sessions with his friends. He also hired the whole of Liberty-Land, the Memphis funfair, in order to ride the dodgems with his friends – again at nighttime or during the early hours of the morning. Another favorite for all-night frolics was the Memphis roller rink, Rainbow Rollerdome, located at 2881 Lamar Avenue.

118

Elvis' sensual good looks were gradually being replaced with bland, plastic handsomeness in a series of increasingly unlikely movies. This resulted in a ludicrous attempt to turn him into a modern Rudolph Valentino in the 1965 Harum Scarum *(bottom).*

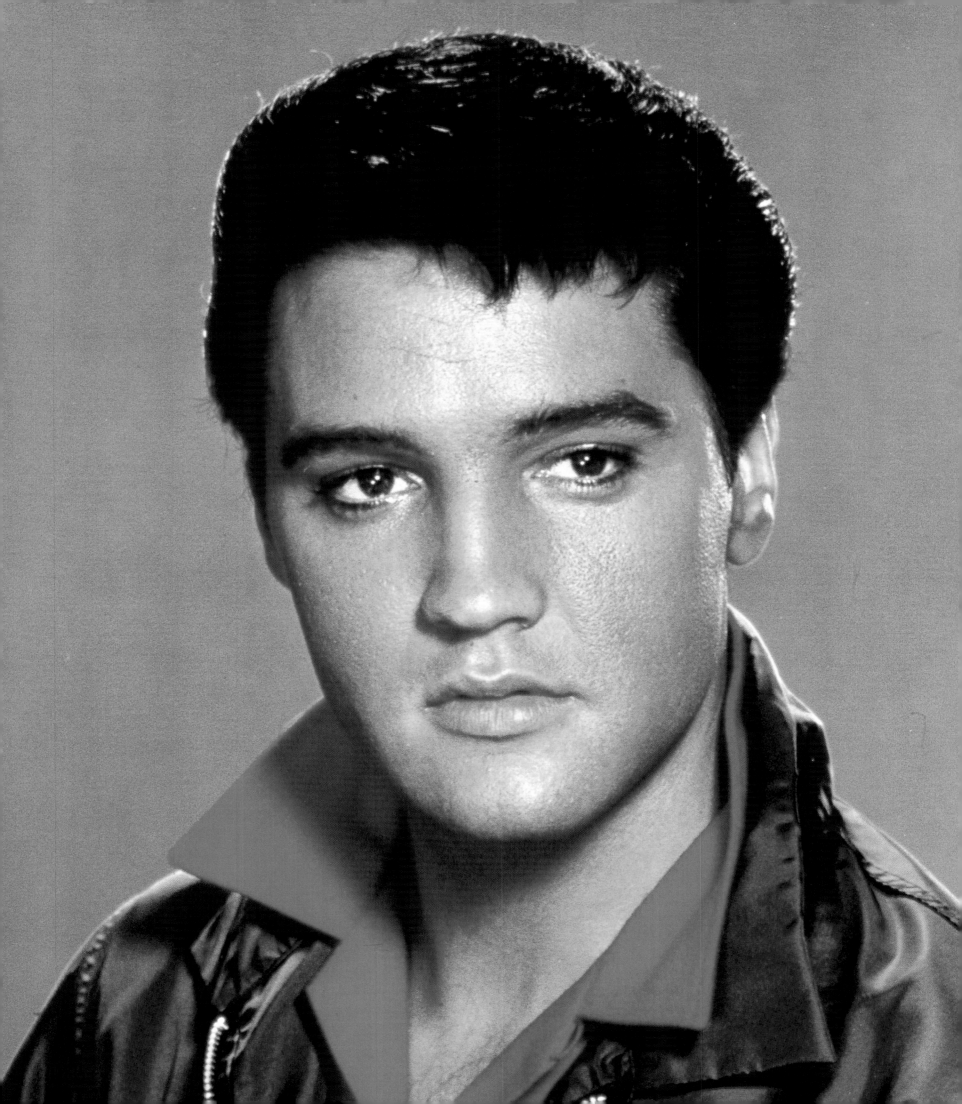

"Plastic man" meets "plastic woman" in Speedway *(1967). The woman is Nancy Sinatra (below), whose father, Frank, had claimed to despise rock-and-roll singers. The setting is an unlikely discotheque with sawed-up cars for booths.* Clambake *(left), is another poor "beach and bikini" movie, set in less exotic Miami Beach, Florida.*

ON MANY OF THESE adventures, Elvis was accompanied by his pet chimpanzee, Scatter, who drank bourbon, rode in the cars, and reportedly pinched girls' behinds.

SOME TIME DURING 1966 Elvis had the Meditation Garden built at the rear of Graceland. The garden was designed for prayer and meditation, and its centerpiece was a statue of Jesus. Elvis used it more frequently as the years went by and his melancholy increased.

THE GENERAL IMPRESSION IS that Elvis was doing no good work during this period. This is hardly the case. While he may have deserted genuine rock-and-roll for movie soundtracks and ballads, he was still producing outstanding work. For instance, in May 1966 he went into the RCA Nashville Studio to record another batch of sacred tunes. The resulting album, *How Great Thou Art*, would be one of the finest of his career, while his rendition of the frequently-recorded title song was possibly the best ever done. (In three minutes, Elvis moves effortlessly from gentle reverence to an operatic climax which, according to one report, even brought tears to the eyes of the recording technicians.) The album won a Grammy for Best Sacred Performance.

NEVERTHELESS, MOST OF HIS work was in trash movies. Another beauty, Shelly Fabares, co-starred in three of these: *Girl Happy* (1964), *Spinout* (1966) and *Clambake* (1967). She became a close friend and one of Elvis' favorite co-stars. Whether or not the relationship deepened into romance is not known, though Priscilla was certainly concerned. One story has it that during the filming of *Spinout*, Elvis and Fabares held a kissing embrace for three minutes after the director called to cut the scene.

BY JUNE, 1967, ELVIS was embarked on another piece of mindless fluff, *Speedway*, which co-starred his friend Nancy Sinatra, who failed to help him prop up the movie. By now, all but the most dedicated fans were staying away from such rubbish.

THE SOUNDTRACK ALBUMS HAD one notable aspect: the so-called "bonus" songs used to pad them out. Usually leftovers from his few studio recording sessions of the period, they included many lovely ballads, spirituals, country tunes and the odd rocker, such as "Blue River" or "Down in the Alley." Best of all was Elvis' definitive interpretation of Bob Dylan's "Tomorrow is a Long Time."

THOUGH REPORTEDLY LOATHING DYLAN'S singing style, Elvis loved his songs.

IN A SURPRISE MOVE, Elvis and Priscilla were married by Nevada Supreme Court Judge David Zenoff, in the Aladdin Hotel, Las Vegas, in the suite of the owner, Milton Prell, on May 1, 1967. Elvis looked plump and sleek, with too much lacquer in his hair, and Priscilla's beauty was lost in heavy makeup and a mane of dyed black hair. Neither looked real.

JOE ESPOSITO AND MARTY LACKER were best men. Priscilla's sister Michele was her maid of honor. Among the other fourteen guests, including the parents

121

Same lips, same eyes, same hair. When Elvis made Priscilla dye her hair black (as he had dyed his own) and use dark mascara, she almost looked like his twin. Appearing alike, they were married at the Aladdin Hotel, Las Vegas, on May 1, 1967. They honeymooned in Palm Springs.

of the bride and groom, were old school buddy George Klein, and Redd Fox, a well-known black comedian and close friend. Not invited were the rest of the Memphis Mafia. This would cause more than a little resentment over the years to come.

ELVIS AND PRISCILLA HONEYMOONED in Palm Springs, then returned to 10050 Rocca Place, Bel Air, where they remained for the first few months of their marriage. Finally, Elvis bought a house: a $400,000 pseudo-French regency mansion located at 1174 Hillcrest Road, in the exclusive Truesdale Estates, Los Angeles. For the rest of his marriage to Priscilla, he commuted between this home and Graceland.

FOR PRISCILLA, THE MARRIAGE did not make life easier. Elvis was still away most of the time, making his movies, and when at home he slept during the day and stayed up all night with the Memphis Mafia, often playing increasingly silly games: shooting light bulbs in the swimming pool; squirting water at one another, passing girls around, popping pills.

THERE WAS LITTLE PRIVACY for Priscilla since, apart from the Memphis Mafia, she had the Graceland staff to contend with, including cooks, secretaries,

123

chauffeurs, valets, maids, gardeners, security guards, beauticians, and various human oddities, such as Elvis' "beautician" and "spiritual advisor" Larry Geller. There were also some long-term relatives, such as grandmother Minnae Mae Presley, as well as Vernon, his wife Dee, and their three sons.

PRISCILLA ALSO HAD PROBLEMS with Elvis' increasing need to shower expensive presents on all and sundry: heaps of flowers from Burke's Florist at 1609 Elvis Presley Boulevard; jewelry from Lowell Hays and Harry Levitch; and even automobiles – he gave cars to adults as casually as giving toys to children, most purchased from Madison Cadillac, in Memphis.

WHEN NOT DISTRACTING HIMSELF by spending money, Elvis was attempting to do so with long periods of meditation in his bedroom, alleged "conversations" with his dead mother and twin brother, the study of esoteric religions and philosophies, and the bedding of visiting fans and other ladies. Priscilla also noticed that the taking of Benzedrine, first begun in Germany, had now led to the necessity for a constant supply of uppers and downers. Elvis was rarely without some tablets by his bedside and was starting to read books about pharmaceutical drugs. Naturally, Priscilla was worried.

BY THE END OF 1967, Elvis was no longer viewed as an exciting talent, but as a spent force and boring, solid citizen. Indeed, among the many awards he had won for his music, there were also awards for his "Americanism," "charity," and "humanity." Unfortunately, he hadn't had a number one record in more than five years, and his last gold record (for sales over a million) was for "Wooden Heart," a rehashed German folk song included in *GI Blues* and first released in 1960. The only other gold record of this period was for "Crying in the Chapel," which was also recorded in 1960. His only albums of the period, apart from the soundtracks and gospel albums, were *Something for Everyone* (1961) and *Elvis for Everyone* (1965), both padded out with old tracks and otherwise perfectly routine. As for his latest movies, though they were still making money they were reviled by critics and fans alike.

CLEARLY, IT WAS TIME for some changes.

ON FEBRUARY 1, 1968, a daughter was born to Elvis and Priscilla in the Baptist Memorial Hospital, located at 899 Madison Avenue, Memphis. She was born nine months to the day after the marriage. The child was named Lisa Marie in honor of Marie Parker, the Colonel's modest, good-humored wife.

THE BIRTH OF LISA MARIE is often credited with spurring a proud Elvis back to work, but more likely it was the knowledge that Priscilla was pregnant that actually got him going.

INDICATIONS THAT HE WAS returning to form came months before the birth of Lisa Marie – with "Guitar Man," a talking country blues on which the song's composer, Jerry "Reed" Hubbard, and steel-guitar player "Sneaky" Peter Drake, provide irresistible licks and rhythms. This minor classic was recorded in

124

Although Priscilla was a natural beauty who required no make-up, Elvis encouraged her to bury her fine features in a mass of dark hair and matching mascara. Nine months to the day after their marriage, on February 1, 1968, Priscilla gave birth to their only child, Lisa Marie (right), in the Baptist Memorial Hospital in Memphis. This was to rejuvenate an artistically jaded Elvis.

September, 1967, at RCA Nashville Studios. It was released as a single with "High-Heel Sneakers" on the flip-side. The latter is a bluesy rocker with pounding bass, great harmonica playing by Charlie McCoy, discordant back-up vocals, and a hoarse-voiced, threatening vocal by Elvis. Also recorded during this session, with some ballads and country songs, was a rollicking version of "Big Boss Man." Other musicians included Scotty Moore, D.J. Fontana, Floyd Cramer, Boots Randolph on saxophone, Charlie McCoy on harmonica, and the Jordanaires and Millie Kirkham on back-up vocals.

While Elvis movies such as Speedway (below) were not improving, the star was looking even more handsome. In subsequent movies, though most remained fairly worthless, he became notably looser and more good-humored.

Inspired by the birth of his daughter, Lisa Marie, Elvis made plans for some decent employment. The new work overlapped with a flurry of activity on what would be the last of his feature films, but these at least show the gradual change in his image. In The Trouble with Girls [And How to Get into it] *(right) and* Change of Habit *(below), both produced in 1968, the year of his legendary NBC-TV Special, Elvis has regrown his sideburns and looks sensually handsome and dangerous. This more mature, sexy Elvis would take the world by storm when he made his first live appearance on television for eight years.*

ON OCTOBER 18, 1967, Elvis began work on *Stay Away, Joe*, a quirky little Western comedy in which he plays a contemporary Navajo Indian brave who smokes, drinks, jokes, sings, fights and does a lot of womanizing. An amiable mess of a movie, it fired no sparks at the box office. In March, 1968, Elvis started work on another movie, *Live a Little, Love a Little*. Though somewhat nonsensical, it was notable for again showing him with sideburns and actually romping (though fully clothed) on a bed with his leading lady, Michele Carey. This was followed all too quickly by *Charro* (1968), a poor attempt at a spaghetti Western, with Elvis grimly impersonating Clint Eastwood. Though the movie was dead on its feet, the unshaven Elvis looked good. In October, production began on the equally inane *The Trouble with Girls [And How to Get into it]* (1968), in which Elvis was hardly more than a "guest" star, not appearing until about forty minutes into the movie. Yet again he was sporting his sideburns and looked slim and incredibly handsome in a snow-white suit.

ELVIS' FINAL ACTING ROLE was in *Change of Habit*, which began production on October 15, 1968. Another attempt at a "serious" movie, it had a good-looking, sideburned Elvis as a doctor in an urban ghetto, falling in love with a nun, played by Mary Tyler Moore. While scarcely credible, it showed again, but alas too late, that Elvis could act.

THOUGH MOST OF THESE final movies were fairly dire, they also gave clear indication that Elvis was attempting to change his ways. The real resurrection came at nine in the evening on Tuesday, December 3, 1968, when a slim, impossibly handsome Elvis, dressed entirely in black except for a blood red 'kerchief around his neck, glared threateningly out of television sets all over the United States and snarled, "If you're lookin' for trouble, you've come to the right place ...."

WHAT FOLLOWED WAS SIXTY minutes of pure gold as a revitalized Elvis, on the NBC-TV Special produced and directed by Steve Binder, went back to his roots, took full measure of his own achievements, and redrew the map of his whole career. Wearing black leather and playing a mean guitar in a jam session with Scotty Moore and J.D. Fontana, Elvis sang his old songs, including "Lawdy Miss Clawdy" and "One Night," with more passion than he had ever shown before. In spectacular set pieces, with full orchestra and teams of dancers, he reproduced the better moments of his movie career. Finally, wearing a snow-white suit and looking other-worldly, he climaxed the show with a hoarse-voiced, deeply-moving rendition of a song written especially for him: "If I Can Dream." That song was rushed out as a single and sold a million in no time.

OVERNIGHT, ELVIS WAS BACK with the world at his feet: the King had reclaimed his crown.

The King Returns

"There have been pretenders. There have been *con*-tenders. But there is only one King."

Bruce Springsteen

I N JANUARY 1969, WITH the NBC-TV Special behind him, the soundtrack album at number eight on the LP charts, and the single "If I Can Dream" climbing the singles charts, Elvis began a lengthy recording session at American Recording in Memphis. This was the first time he had recorded in Memphis since leaving Sun for RCA in 1955.

AMERICAN RECORDING WAS THEN the most successful studio in the country, with most of its records produced by Chips Moman. It was also renowned for its exceptional house band, consisting mostly of white southerners who had been inspired by Elvis and specialized in blues-based "soul" music. From one session that should have been ten days, but was reduced to six because Elvis contracted laryngitis, Elvis and his dedicated band produced at least twenty-one tracks. ("Lost" tracks have popped up over the years since then.) At a second session in February, when Elvis had recovered, they produced another fourteen – a total of thirty-five, covering everything from Burt Bacharach to gospel, soul, country, the blues, mainstream pop, social comment, and some that defied categorization. Four became Top Ten singles and a considerable number were outstanding album tracks, to be found on *From Elvis in Memphis* and the studio disk of the *From Memphis to Vegas/From Vegas to Memphis* double set. The singles included "In the Ghetto," Mac Davis' unforgettable ballad about the birth, life and death of a poor urban black man; and "Suspicious Minds" an Elvis masterpiece and the last number one of his career.

ALL IN ALL, IT was one of the most remarkable recording sessions in the history of popular music.

"ELVIS WAS SUPERNATURAL, HIS OWN RESURRECTION, AT THE SHOWROOM INTERNATIONAL IN LAS VEGAS."
David Dalton, *Rolling Stone*

"I WATCHED THE AUDIENCE AS HE WALKED OUT ON STAGE, AND SO MANY HAD THEIR FACES IN THEIR HANDS. THEY'D SIT THERE AND CRY. IT WAS ALMOST BIBLICAL, AS IF THE CLOUDS HAD PARTED AND DOWN A SHAFT OF LIGHT CAME THE ANGELS."
Bill Jost, Assistant Maitre d', Showroom of International Hotel, Las Vegas

BY THIS TIME COLONEL PARKER had signed a deal with Kirk Kerkorian, owner of the International Hotel in Las Vegas, for Elvis to play the hotel's 2600-seat Showroom, following hot on the heels of Barbara Streisand, who had opened the building a month earlier. Elvis would receive $1 million for a four-week engagement; an unprecedented sum in those days.

ELVIS' FIRST LIVE APPEARANCE in eight years took place on July 31, 1969. No longer would he appear with just a guitarist, bass player and drummer. Backing him this time were southern blues guitarist James Burton, ace drummer Ronnie Tutt, bassist Jerry Scheff, keyboard player Larry Muhoberac, and guitarists John Wilkinson and Charlie Hodge, who also supplied vocal harmonies. Further vocal back-up was provided by two groups. The first was the Sweet Inspirations, including Myrna Smith, Estelle Brown, Sylvia Stenwell and Cissy Houston, who had previously sung with Aretha Franklin and Ricky Nelson, as well as having their own 1968 Atlantic hit, "Sweet Inspiration." Not content with these fine ladies, Elvis also employed Kathy Westmoreland, whom he was often to introduce as "the little lady with the high voice." To this large contingent of female voices, Elvis added the Stamps Quartet, led by J.D. Sumner ("the most celebrated bass voice in gospel music") and including Donnie Sumner, Bill Blaize, Ed Enoch, Richard Staborn and, later, Ed Wideman. Last, but not least, was a full-scale orchestra, including brass and string sections, composed and conducted by Joe Guercio.

IN THE AUDIENCE FOR the opening show were soundtrack composer Henry Mancini, Cary Grant, Sammy Davis Jr., Tom Jones, Juliet Prowse, Fats Domino, Pat

132

Boone, numerous other stars of stage and screen and, of course, Vernon, Priscilla, Colonel Parker, the Memphis Mafia, and even Sam Phillips.

WHEN THE BAND OPENED with a pounding rock-and-roll intro, a darkly handsome, slim Elvis emerged wearing a black, modified karate suit with trim, slashed to the waist, a striped 'kerchief, high heels, and a guitar. Before he could begin, the roaring of the audience stopped him dead. When the bedlam had died down, he launched into "Blue Suede Shoes," followed it with a blistering "I Got a Woman," then drove his audience wild with a selection that covered everything from the early Sun days to his great RCA rockers, a couple of Beatles' songs, Chuck Berry, and some of his own recent hits. Not content with this, he laid them to waste with an astonishing, six-minute version of "Suspicious Minds," concluded with "Can't Help Falling in Love," and returned for the only encore of his career in the form of a blistering work-out on Ray Charles' "What'd I Say?" He still moved all over the place, but his early hip-swinging gyrations had been replaced with more precise, graceful, equally exciting body movements based on his karate exercises.

THE AUDIENCE WAS ECSTATIC and the critics raved. "Supernatural," said *Rolling Stone*. "Incredible," said *Newsweek*. Performing twice a night for four weeks, Elvis resurrected all the glories of his past, regained his whole domain, and broke every Las Vegas attendance record.

SIX MONTHS LATER, IN January 1970, he returned, this time wearing a tassled white jumpsuit, to give a slicker show, with less pure rock-and-roll, though he topped his audacious six-minute "Suspicious Minds" with a definitive, gyrating rendition of Tony Joe White's swamp-rock epic, "Polk Salad Annie."

SHOOTING OF A DOCUMENTARY based on the concerts commenced during his third season at Las Vegas, in July 1970, and included footage shot in Phoenix, Arizona, the following September, during the first of what would be many concert tours organized by Jerry Weintraub's Concerts West organization.

THE RESULTANT MOVIE, *That's the Way it is* (1970), if nearly ruined by some dreadful "fan" interviews, was a treat for the thousands of fans living outside America and, incidentally, an exciting record of the "live" Elvis at his peak.

THE TRIUMPHANT RETURN OF the man now known simply as "The King" was climaxed on January 9, 1971, when Elvis was awarded by the U.S. Jaycees as one of "The Ten Outstanding Young Men of America." In February, Britain's *New Musical Express* named him the world's top male singer for the twelfth time in thirteen years. He also won the Bing Crosby Award of the National Academy of Arts and Sciences – the highest award in music – for his "outstanding creative and artistic contributions of long-lasting duration in the field of phonograph recordings."

IT WAS A REMARKABLE year by any standard of achievement, but from here on it would mostly be downhill.

ELVIS HAD CONQUERED AMERICA not only once, but twice, and now he had nothing else to do. As with many another enormously talented artist, as soon as

134

Elvis was partly stung into returning to live performances by seeing the Las Vegas show of the dynamic British singer, Tom Jones (above). The other motivation was, of course, his daughter Lisa Marie, shown at the top of this page and with Elvis and Priscilla (right).

The first couple of years of Elvis' return to live performances showed him to be the most exciting performer in show business. Unfortunately, this dazzling return to form would be short-lived.

he had proved himself he lost interest again, and what had been a challenge became a chore. Just as a combination of exploitative management and Elvis' own indifference had led to a decade of bad movies with recycled plots, so the same attitudes now led to a gross capitalization on his new reputation as an outstanding live performer, with endless tours of the United States (two shows a day, sometimes even three), a string of "live" albums, and the recycling of old material instead of badly needed new recordings.

THE RESULTS SOON SHOWED in the declining quality of his recorded output and indifferent performances onstage, where grandiose rhinestone jump-suits and diamond-studded belts (all designed by Bill Belew, who had created the sensational black leather outfit worn by Elvis for his 1968 Christmas Singer Special NBC-TV comeback show) covered up for the lack of splendor in his work.

NOT THAT IT WAS all dross. "Don't Cry Daddy," his follow-up single to the blockbusting "Suspicious Minds," became another million seller. This was followed by a powerhouse ballad, "The Wonder of You," taken off the excellent "live" album, *On Stage*, and released in May 1970, a month before the album release. A marathon recording session in June produced a staggering thirty-four tracks, ranging from the excellent to the awful. The decline in quality was due not only to the sheer amount of material recorded too quickly, but to the fact that Elvis had already forsaken American Recording in Memphis for RCA Nashville, lost some of his best rock musicians, such as Scotty Moore, D.J. Fontana, Bob Moore and Buddy Harman, and was concentrating on often old-fashioned ballads. Nevertheless, the session produced two million-selling albums, *That's the Way it*

A slim, confident Elvis gives a rare press conference following his triumphant opening show in Las Vegas in August, 1969.

is (a mixture of studio and live recordings) and the classic, *Elvis Country*, as well as one Top Ten hit and a number of smaller hits.

BY MAY 15 THE following year, when Elvis returned to Nashville for another marathon recording session to include songs for a Christmas album, the drugs had made him more hot-tempered, autocratic, disinterested, and generally unpredictable. Also, according to drummer Jerry Carrigan, everybody was drinking and "going outside and smoking dope." More than once Elvis lost his temper and stormed from the studio. Nevertheless, at the various sessions conducted between May and June, another large batch of tracks was laid down.

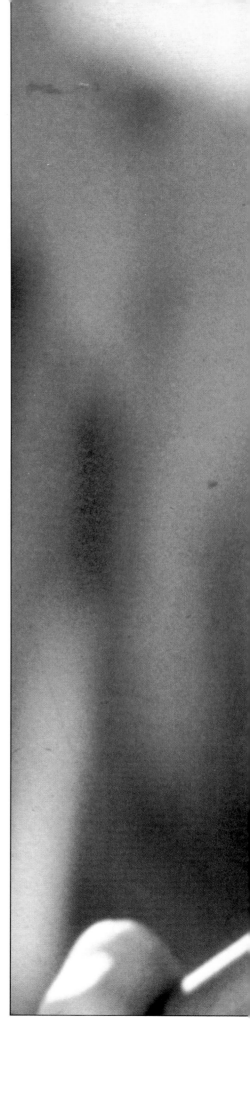

THE SESSIONS PRODUCED THE expected Christmas album, *Elvis Sings the Wonderful World of Christmas*, and the gospel album, *He Touched Me*. While both contained good individual tracks, overall there was a sad decline in quality. The lackluster Christmas album is redeemed by a terrific five-minute blues, "Merry Christmas Baby" and the bluesy ballad, "I'll be Home on Christmas Day." The gospel album is much better, but certainly not up to the quality of his previous work in this field. Nevertheless, it won him another Grammy.

THE SAME SESSION PRODUCED the second of the only two Bob Dylan songs recorded by Elvis: "Don't Think Twice, It's All Right" – actually a great warm-up jam – and "I'm Leaving," one of the finest, sadly overlooked, singles of his later period.

IN 1971 THE TEN-MILE stretch of US Highway 51 South that passes Graceland was named "Elvis Presley Boulevard" in honor of the city's most famous son. However, such honors notwithstanding, it was clear to those with eyes and ears that Elvis was becoming unstable. His increasing dependence on amphetamines and barbiturates (uppers and downers) was making him leap dangerously between acute highs, serious lows, and violent outbursts of temper.

TRYING TO STAY IN control, he concentrated even more on his karate, taking personal instructions in Kempo from Hawaiian-born expert Ed Parker and another expert, Mike Stone. Unfortunately, the latter fell in love with Priscilla, thus hastening the break between her and Elvis.

The revitalized Elvis dazzled critics and audiences alike. His youthful leg-shaking and hip-swivelling had been replaced by body movements that combined grace with power and were driven by a flawless sense of rhythm. Much of this came from karate, which Elvis had practiced constantly since his stint with the army, and continued until almost the very end. His clever utilization of various karate movements in his stage act made him even more impressive.

140

If Elvis was still exciting on stage and seemed to be a happy man, his constant touring was placing a strain on his marriage and Priscilla, though smiling in public, was not very happy.

PRISCILLA HAD BECOME DISENCHANTED with her life at Graceland; particularly with Elvis' growing drug dependence, his increasingly bizarre behavior, and his refusal, or inability, to make love to her. Eventually, it became too much and she looked for comfort elsewhere. She found it with Mike Stone and subsequently left Graceland, and Elvis, for good on February 23, 1972.

ELVIS WAS DEEPLY SHOCKED, viewing her departure and the loss of Lisa Marie as the greatest blow since the death of his mother.

HE NEVER FULLY RECOVERED. From this point on he would concentrate more on recording semi-autobiographical ballads of lost love than on rock songs — though not before producing one final rock-and-roll classic.

IN MARCH, 1972, AT the MGM Recording Studio, Los Angeles, during one of his typically long, unfocused recording sessions, he laid down "Burning Love."

141

Once Elvis left Las Vegas and took to the road, his performances began to lose their luster. His voice was unimpaired and the audiences were still ecstatic, but his health was deteriorating, his weight was increasing, and the dynamics of his earlier perform-ances were being replaced with ever more elaborate costumes, grandiose orchestral arrange-ments, and some pointless fooling around. Nevertheless, he still seemed increasingly god-like.

This blistering rocker, noted for the dynamic drumming of Ronnie Tutt and the guitars of James Burton and John Wilkinson, allowed Elvis to give full expression to lyrics saturated in sexual innuendo. ("I'm just a hunk, a hunk of burning love ....") Released as a single in August 1972, it reached number two on *Billboard's* Hot 100 Chart and remained there for approximately fifteen weeks to compensate Elvis for a long, barren period and remind his fans that he still had the talent, if rarely the inclination, to deliver the goods.

ALAS, HE WOULD NOT repeat the performance, though his talent was far from diminished. "Burning Love" was followed by a single containing two sides beloved by the fans: "Separate Ways" and "You Were Always on my Mind." Both were anthems for his failed marriage to Priscilla. (The former was written by Red West.) While they were ballads of high quality, with deeply felt vocals, they were also sad indications of the course his future recordings would take: the confessional ballad.

A MONTH LATER, ELVIS was on the road again. For these shows he supplemented the Sweet Inspirations and the Stamps with a third vocal back-up

143

group, Voice, to create an even more grandiose sound. Voice consisted of Sherril Nielson, one of the greatest living Irish tenors, with Tim Batey and Donnie Sumner, who had moved over to the new group from the Stamps Quartet.

THIS TOUR LED TO the movie, *Elvis on Tour* (1972), produced and directed by Pierre Adidge and Robert Abel. In this documentary Elvis is more bloated and less concerned with his appearance than he was in *That's the Way it is*. Also, his voice is showing distinct signs of wear and tear. Nevertheless, his energy and sense of humor are intact, the performances are shot with an exciting use of multiple-images, the backstage scenes are less controlled, thus infinitely more involving, and, as an unprecedented bonus, a lengthy taped interview between Elvis and the producers/directors gives a tantalizing glimpse into the former's attitude to his early body movements, guitar-playing and gospel singing.

THE MOVIE WON A Golden Globe award for best documentary.

ELVIS' BIGGEST CHALLENGE IN 1972 was his appearance at New York's Madison Square Garden on June 10. Although the Garden was then noted for having the toughest, most sophisticated audiences in America, Elvis took the venue by storm and conquered the city.

AN ALBUM OF THE complete evening show, *Elvis as Recorded at Madison Square Garden*, was released only eight days later and went on to sell over a million, despite the fact that most of the songs had been heard before. Unfortunately, the huge sales only reinforced the belief of Colonel Parker and RCA that the release of such albums, which were virtually all the same, was a way of making quick, easy money.

ELVIS WAS NOW USING the lightweight comedian Jackie Kahane to warm up his audience and announce the end of the show. (Apart from his first night at Las Vegas in 1970, Elvis never took encores.) Kahane is now most famous for his often repeated announcement: "Ladies and gentlemen, Elvis has left the building."

ON JANUARY 8, 1973, on his 38th birthday, Elvis filed for divorce from Priscilla. On the 14th he returned to Hawaii to do the *Aloha From Hawaii* satellite show, in aid of the Kui Lee Cancer Drive. (Kui Lee was the Hawaiian singer and composer of "I'll Remember You." He died of cancer in 1966.) The performance at the Honolulu International Center Arena was broadcast by Intelsat TV satellite and viewed simultaneously by more than one billion people in over forty countries, thus making it another world record-breaker for the alarmingly remote, bleary-eyed, yet still mesmerizing performer.

A POWERHOUSE OPENING OF "See See Rider" and "Burning Love" was followed by a lengthy selection of old hits and new offerings. Most of the other rock songs in the selection were performed in a perfunctory manner, with the exception of an electrifying "Steamroller Blues." However, many of the ballads compensated for this, including the impassioned "You Gave Me a Mountain," the beautiful "It's Over," and the heartfelt "I'm so Lonesome I Could Cry." Undoubtedly

Elvis, magnificent in the "Aloha From Hawaii Via Satellite" TV broadcast (right), but his dulled gaze (below), told a sadder story.

"I SAW HIM AT THE GARDEN. HE WAS IN GOOD SHAPE, LOOKED REAL GOOD .... I FELT WONDERFUL WHEN HE SANG 'BRIDGE OVER TROUBLED WATER,' EVEN THOUGH IT WAS A TOUCH ON THE DRAMATIC SIDE – BUT SO WAS THE SONG."
Paul Simon

these were aided by the pain Elvis was suffering because of the ongoing divorce proceedings.

THERE IS A CERTAIN poignancy in the fact that in this concert Elvis first performed "My Way," the Paul-Anka-penned Frank Sinatra hit that became Elvis' way of informing his fans that he was deeply unhappy.

NO MEAN MAN COULD steal a song from Sinatra, but Elvis did just that.

THE DOUBLE ALBUM OF the concert, *Aloha From Hawaii Via Satellite*, though only containing eight new songs in a total of twenty-three, went on to sell over two million units. Unfortunately, these phenomenal sales merely confirmed for all concerned that live albums, no matter how lackluster, could make as much money as carefully-wrought studio recordings.

WHEN NOT RELEASING SUCH albums, RCA were pushing out a stream of lucrative repackages: a four-disk box set, *Elvis: Worldwide 50 Gold Award Hits, Volume 1*, complete with picture book, remained on *Billboard's* bestselling charts for almost six months. Its successor, another 4-box set, *Elvis: The Other Sides,*

Worldwide Gold Hits, Volume II, sold almost as well, despite its high cost. These were followed by some exploitative compilations, such as *Burning Love and Hits from his Movies*. On this, the only "hit" is "Burning Love."

ON JULY 21, 1973, Elvis recorded for the last time in Memphis. He arrived at Stax Studio wearing a long black cape, white suit and "Superfly" hat. The musicians were forced to hang around, doing nothing, while the disinterested singer played through stacks of demonstration disks of possible songs. One of the songs was so bad that the studio drummer, Al Jackson, refused to play on it. Elvis recorded little during the first five days, and did not turn up at all on the sixth and seventh. That session, and another one in the same studio in December, produced enough tracks for a couple of mediocre albums.

BY 1975 ELVIS WAS recording his vocals separately and sending them to RCA Studios, Hollywood, to have the music and back-up vocals overdubbed in his absence. Toward the end, he was recording, with lamentable results, in the basement of Graceland.

Even as the excellent documentary Elvis: That's the Way it is *(1970) was being released to show the fans worldwide how dynamic Elvis could be on stage, he was starting to throw it all away. These photos (above and right) are reminders of how exciting Elvis was before the deterioration set in.*

AT THE DIVORCE PROCEEDINGS on October 11, 1973, in the Superior Court of Santa Monica, Priscilla was represented by Los Angeles attorney Robert Brock. The divorce was granted by Judge Laurence J. Rittenband.

WHEN PRISCILLA WAS GRANTED custody of Lisa Marie, Elvis agreed that this was correct. In return, Priscilla was generous with visiting privileges, allowing Lisa Marie to spend part of her summer vacations with Elvis, as well as visiting on many other occasions. Elvis adored Lisa Marie and doted on her. He also missed her deeply when she was away, and was constantly fearful of kidnappers; a concern that would grow into paranoia during his last years.

MONEY RAISED ITS UGLY head only briefly. Following the initial settlement, Priscilla claimed that Elvis had failed to disclose his true financial assets. She brought suit for extrinsic fraud and the final settlement made her wealthy overnight. Apart from this brief conflict, she and Elvis remained good friends.

NEVERTHELESS, THOUGH STILL SEEING Priscilla and Lisa Marie, Elvis was in despair. He found consolation with another beauty queen, Linda Diane Thompson, the former "Miss Tennessee," who became his live-in companion and traveling girlfriend for about four years.

BY THIS TIME HE certainly needed a traveling companion, as he was pressed by Colonel Parker into another grueling series of tours, during which he performed with increasing indifference or eccentricity, often fooling around on stage or offering bizarre, interminable monologues rather than singing.

TO ELVIS' DISGUST, COLONEL PARKER put some of the recorded monologues onto a very bad "all talking" album, *Having Fun with Elvis on Stage*. He released it, without Elvis' permission, on his own Boxcar label.

BY 1974 ELVIS WAS so doped-up and bloated he was falling out of his limousine, holding onto the mike for support, and slurring so badly that the words of the songs could scarcely be made out. During his performance at the University of Maryland in College Park, on September 27, he was in such bad shape that conductor Joe Guercio was reduced to tears. At Greensboro, on July 21, he was so insulting to his back-up singers that Kathy Westmoreland and two of the Sweet Inspirations walked off stage. Elvis, now adrift in his drugged world, appeared not to notice.

DURING THE LAST YEARS of his life, Elvis was heavily into the reading of books on religion, philosophy, psychology, and medicine. These included Kahlil Gibran's *The Prophet*, Paramahansa Yogananda's *Autobiography of a Yogi*, Krishnamurti's *The First and Last Freedom*, Cheiro's *Book of Numbers*, Manley Palmer Hall's *The Mystical Christ*, Joel Goldsmith's *The Infinite Way*, Baird Spalding's *The Life and Teachings of the Master of the Far East*, and the works of Madame Blavatsky, Albert Pike, May Heindel, and Nicholas Roerich. Perhaps because Christ and a few of Elvis' ancestors were Jewish, he also developed a growing interest in Judaism, studying the *Dead Sea Scrolls* and the Hebrew *Cabala*.

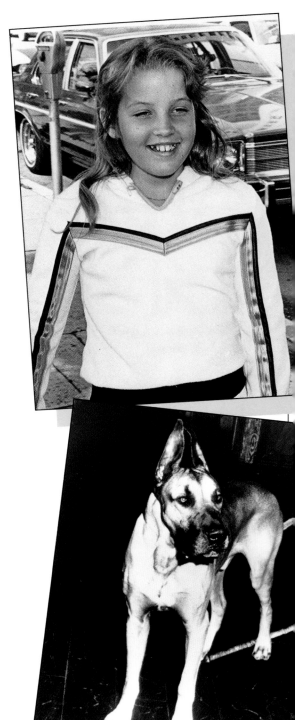

One of Elvis' many pet dogs, Snoopy (above) became Lisa Marie's constant companion at Graceland. Sadly, on October 11, 1973, Elvis and Priscilla were divorced at Santa Monica Superior Court (right).

151

Elvis' life at Graceland with his Memphis Mafia had always been bizarre, but became even more so after his divorce from Priscilla. His interest in guns began early and was at first merely a boyish enthusiasm, leading to an excellent collection of old and new weapons. However, as the years went by, this innocent interest merged unhealthily with a growing obsession with law and order – ironically including drug-busting. The games played by Elvis and the Memphis Mafia were often childish (playing cops and robbers with pistols) and sometimes merely foolish (shooting lightbulbs floating in the swimming pool). But some activities were more dangerous (shooting out of switched-on television sets).

Two "Nixons" were instrumental in encouraging Elvis to play more serious "cops and robbers." One was Richard Nixon, the 37th president of the United States, who received an unexpected visit from the legendary star on December 21, 1970, and was charmed into making him a federal narcotic's agent. The other was Memphis Sheriff Roy Nixon, shown behind Elvis, under the wreath (bottom left). He swore in Elvis and his good ol' boys as deputies, allowing them to pull in any drivers suspected of being drug dealers.

The men in the Memphis Mafia picture (bottom left) standing from left to right are: Billy Smith, Bill Morris, Lamar Fike, Jerry Schilling, Memphis Sheriff Roy Nixon, Vernon Presley, Charlie Hodge, Sonny West, George Klein, and Marty Lacker. Kneeling to Elvis' right is the soon-to-be-notorious Dr. George Nichopoulos and to Elvis' left is Red West. Red and his brother Sonny would soon be collaborating with Steve Dunleavy on the notorious exposé, Elvis: What Happened? *For this act of treachery, Elvis fans worldwide would classify the former friends and bodyguards as Judases.*

Reportedly, on the day he died, he was reading *The Force of Jesus* by Frank Adams.

ELVIS WAS ALSO OBSESSED with guns and made frequent visits to Charles Church's law enforcement accessories shop and nearby shooting range in Whitehaven. Church was responsible for supplying and installing the multi-camera, closed-circuit video monitoring system at Graceland.

ELVIS' GROWING DRUG ADDICTION and obsession with Law and Order had made him, in 1971, embark on a crazed journey to Washington D.C., where he presented himself at the White House and obtained an audience with the President, Richard Nixon. Contradicting a previous refusal by Deputy Director John Finlater, the 37th President of the United States personally made Elvis a federal narcotics agent, thus proving that American politics is even crazier than show business. Not satisfied, Elvis then persuaded Nixon to meet his buddies, Jerry Schilling and Sonny West, and also present them with official drug squad badges. Then he flew back to Memphis in his private plane, to be made a private deputy by Sheriff Roy Nixon of Memphis.

HE CONTINUED SHOWERING THE Memphis Mafia and others with extravagant gifts, and in one instance, in July 1975, purchased fourteen Eldorado cars in a single day. In return for this generosity, he was called "Boss," "Chief," "the Big E" and "Crazy" by his entourage. His fans were now calling him "E.P.," "Pres.," or simply "The King." Small wonder Elvis developed messianic complexes and, towards the end, began to confuse himself with his Maker and became impossible to deal with.

153

When not firing off his guns, overeating or popping pills, the increasingly bloated Elvis entertained himself in other ways. His motorcycle collection included many Harley Davidsons (left), and he also enjoyed driving around the grounds of Graceland in go-carts, sometimes teasing the fans by driving outside (below). When performing, he tried to hide his growing weight with his ever more elaborate jumpsuits; but overweight or not, he still managed to look bizarrely magnificent (right).

Despite his personal problems Elvis kept touring, though the relentless pace was taking its toll. From the slim, triumphant Elvis of 1970 (left), to the heavy-lidded, remote Elvis of 1973 (below) and the bloated, slowed down, but still beloved Elvis of 1976, the signs of deterioration were unavoidable.

"HE WAS PRETTY MUCH THE SAME THE LAST TIME I SAW HIM AND THE FIRST TIME I SAW HIM. I LAST PLAYED WITH HIM ON JULY 4TH, 1976, FOR THE BICENTENNIAL IN MEMPHIS. HE DIDN'T HARDLY MOVE AS MUCH AS HE USED TO – I THINK IT WAS THE OVERWEIGHT PROBLEM. BUT HE TURNED THE CROWD ON JUST THE SAME. HE NEVER CHANGED; HE JUST POLISHED WHAT HE STARTED WITH. BUT HE ALWAYS HAD IT."
Carl Perkins

IN MAY 1975, ELVIS gave another benefit show in Jackson, Mississippi, this time to help recent tornado victims. In fact, he should have thrown a benefit for himself, since, although he had earned over a hundred million dollars, his extravagant lifestyle had made him almost broke.

ALSO, IN FEBRUARY 1975, when Elvis was actually in hospital having tests on an enlarged colon, drug detoxication, glaucoma, and liver damage caused by the drug abuse, Vernon had a severe heart attack, reputedly brought on by the strain of trying to cope with his son's bizarre behavior. After a period in the hospital's intensive care unit, Vernon was moved into the suite next to Elvis. Elvis was checked out first, but then had to go back to visit Vernon.

THAT SAME YEAR, VERNON and Dee split up.

BY 1976, ELVIS' BEHAVIOR on stage and in the recording studios had lost him most of the leading members of his band: pianist Glenn D. Hardin, his replacement David Briggs, drummer Ronnie Tutt, even lead guitarist James Burton. In July, following the resignation or dismissal of most of the Memphis Mafia, Vernon, who had always viewed the gang members as leeches, dismissed Elvis' troublesome bodyguards, Dave Hebler and Red and Sonny West. These former friends retaliated by making a deal with the *National Star* to expose Elvis in a paperback book. Shortly after, Linda Thompson split from Elvis and took up with David Briggs.

A BLOATED, WEARY ELVIS made his last appearance before an audience at the Market Square Arena, Indiana, on July 26, 1977.

BY THIS TIME IT WAS clear to many that his health was deteriorating as his weight increased. During the seventies he had frequently been admitted to the

Baptist Memorial Hospital on Madison Avenue, Memphis (where Lisa Marie had been born) for health and drug-related problems. The first known visit was in October, 1973. There were more visits between January and February of 1975, then again in August and September. By 1977 he was back in hospital.

ON AUGUST 2, 1977, BALLANTINE BOOKS, New York, shocked Elvis and most of the English-speaking world with the release of *Elvis: What Happened?* This book, known to many contemptuous fans as "the bodyguard book," was put together by Australian hack Steve Dunleavy from the resentful reminiscences of Elvis' brutally dismissed Memphis Mafia bodyguards, David Hebler and Red and Jimmy West. The book revealed that Elvis took drugs in huge quantities, engaged in some unsavory sexual activities, and had an unwholesome obsession with guns, mortuary corpses, videotaped sex, and the ghosts of his dead mother and twin brother.

WHAT SHOCKED MANY FANS and critics alike, was not the revelations of Elvis' dark side, but the book's deliberate sensationalism and ghoulish concentration on these particular aspects of its unfortunate subject. Dunleavy also outraged many by personally describing Elvis as "white trash."

ELVIS WAS SHOCKED AND dismayed by the book (he had practically begged his old, resentful buddies not to publish it) and many of those who knew him at the time felt that the book was, if not the direct cause, certainly one of the major reasons for what was to come.

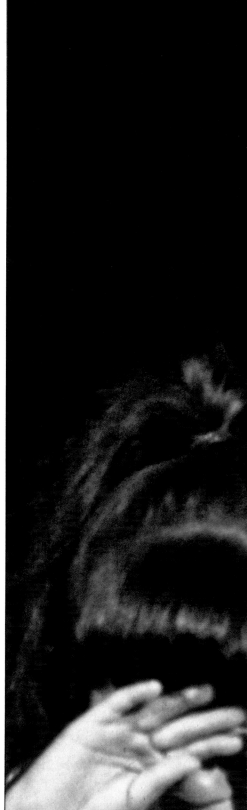

Elvis' introductory music was Richard Strauss' Also sprach Zarathustra *and his striking and colorful appearance increasingly reflected this dramatic introduction.*

Still performing in early 1977 (left), the overweight Elvis remained a striking, handsome figure, though the light in his eyes was focused inward. When not performing painfully, he was being comforted by new girlfriend Ginger Alden, (above), on vacation with Elvis in Kailua, Hawaii, in March 1977. This was Elvis' last year on earth.

BY THIS TIME, ELVIS was involved with live-in girlfriend, Ginger Alden, a nineteen-year-old former "Miss Memphis Traffic Safety," Priscilla look-alike and, ironically, the daughter of Walter Alden, who had inducted Elvis into the army in 1958.

ON AUGUST 16, 1977, fifteen days after the publication of *Elvis: What Happened?*, with Lisa Marie sleeping upstairs in the Graceland mansion, Elvis took a book into the bathroom and did not emerge again. Concerned, Ginger Alden entered the bathroom and found Elvis lying face down on the floor. Thinking he had collapsed, she frantically called Joe Esposito, who tried to give artificial respiration. Failing, Joe called the paramedics from Unit 6 of the Memphis Fire Department. When they, too, failed to revive Elvis, the body was rushed into the Baptist Memorial Hospital. There, a three-hour autopsy was carried out by Dr. Eric Muirhead, while hospital official Maurice Elliot tried to keep the frantic media at bay.

AT EIGHT O'CLOCK THAT EVENING, Elliot announced, officially, that Elvis was dead.

TO ELVIS IN MEMORIAM
YOU GAVE YOURSELF TO EACH OF US IN
SOME MANNER. YOU WERE WRAPPED IN
THOUGHTFULNESS AND TIED WITH LOVE.
MAY THIS FLAME REFLECT OUR NEVER
ENDING RESPECT AND LOVE FOR YOU.
MAY IT SERVE AS A CONSTANT REMINDER
TO EACH OF US OF YOUR ETERNAL
PRESENCE.

ELVIS
AARON
PRESLEY
JANUARY 8, 1935
AUGUST 16, 1977

Death and Resurrection

"Hush, little children, don't you cry
You know your daddy's bound to die
But all my trials, Lord, soon be ended."

An American Trilogy

THE FUNERAL SERVICE FOR Elvis was held in Graceland at two o'clock in the afternoon, on August 18, 1977. Among the 200 people attending were Vernon, Lisa, Priscilla, Linda Thompson, Ginger Alden, actor George Hamilton, a particularly distraught Ann-Margret, her husband Roger Smith, Governor Ray Blanton, and James Brown, the great black rhythm and blues soul performer and admirer of Elvis. Kathy Westmoreland sang "My Heavenly Father," which she had often sung for Elvis onstage; the gospel singer, Jake Hess, one of Elvis' boyhood idols, sang "Known Only to Him," which Elvis had recorded for his gospel album, *His Hand in Mine*; James Blackwood sang "How Great Thou Art," and the Stamps sang "His Hand in Mine" and "Sweet, Sweet Spirit." Eulogies were given by C.W. Bradley, pastor of the Whitehaven Church of Christ; by Rex Humbard, one of Elvis' favorite television preachers; and finally, by comedian Jackie Kahane, who had opened and closed Elvis' concerts during the final years.

THOUSANDS OF FANS HAD gathered outside in mourning. In scenes unparalleled since the death of Valentino, over a thousand security men and police fought to hold back the growing crowds as they attempted to break through the gates and scale the walls. In the grounds of Graceland, an emergency medical center and ten ambulances were attempting to deal with the 300 people who had already fainted or been crushed in the crowd. One woman had gone into labor pains and given birth in an ambulance.

TO ADD TO THE tragedy, two teenage girls who had flown thousands of miles for a final glimpse of Elvis were killed when a car drove into the crowd of mourners. The two girls were killed instantly, another was critically injured, and

"ELVIS WAS THEIR AMERICAN DREAM, THE POOR BOY THAT GOT RICH AND THEY HATED HIM FOR IT. AND THEN HE DIED AND THEY TURNED HIM INTO THIS GOD FORM. AND I THINK THAT'S FASCINATING."
Eddie Murphy, actor

163

the eighteen-year-old driver was charged with second degree murder, drunken driving and leaving the scene of an accident.

AT FOUR O'CLOCK NUMEROUS Cadillacs and other cars made the slow journey along Elvis Presley Boulevard, from Graceland to Forest Hill Cemetery. Elvis' casket was carried in a white Cadillac hearse, past the 150,000 fans and onlookers lining the road. Over 3000 floral tributes in the shape of guitars, hound dogs, crosses and broken hearts covered the lawns of the cemetery. After a short service in the mausoleum, the casket was placed in the crypt. Television coverage and photographs of the complete event swamped the whole world.

A FEW DAYS LATER, the body of Gladys Presley was removed from her plot in Forest Hill Cemetery and placed with Elvis in the family mausoleum.

ON AUGUST 29 RONNIE LEE ADKINS was arrested and charged with attempting to steal Elvis' body from the mausoleum (reportedly with the help of two other men, Raymond Green and Bruce Nelson) in order to "ransom" it. Charges were dismissed, but because of this incident, as well as the predatory activities of many fans, both bodies were moved on October 2 to the Meditation Garden at Graceland.

THE FOLLOWING DAY, OCTOBER 3, CBS-TV aired *Elvis in Concert*, which included performances from his final concert tour (Omaha, Nebraska, on June 19, 1977 and Rapid City, South Dakota, on June 21) and showed a shockingly bloated, dazed Elvis giving a deeply moving rendition of "My Way."

HE HAD SUNG HIS last song.

SHELBY COUNTY CORONER Dr. Jerry Francisco listed the official cause of death as cardiac arrhythmia: an irregular heartbeat resulting from hypertension and other

Hundreds of fans, security men and police surrounded Grace-land the day Elvis died. Below: a fan is doubly shocked after witnessing the death of two girls, killed when a car drove into the crowd of mourners. Right: the funeral procession moves down Elvis Presley Boulevard in Memphis, witnessed by thousands of mourners.

"THE BOOK BY ALBERT GOLDMAN MADE ELVIS OUT AS BEING THE ROCK 'N' ROLL IDIOT. THE BOOK MADE ME VERY, VERY ANGRY. BECAUSE I BELIEVE THAT ELVIS PRESLEY WAS A GENIUS ... "
Bono

factors. No mention was made of drugs. However, analysis of Elvis' body tissue, following the autopsy, was entrusted to the Bio-Sciences Laboratory in Los Angeles and produced traces of eleven different drugs, some of which were narcotics and amphetamines.

IT THEN TRANSPIRED THAT Hollywood private detective John O'Grady (originally hired by Elvis to protect him from paternity suits and death threats, and possibly used in a failed negotiation to stop Red and Sonny West from publishing

Even as thousands of fans were filing through the flower-strewn grounds and rooms of Graceland to view Elvis' body, rumors were circulating that Elvis' heart attack had been caused by his addiction to pharmaceutical drugs. Soon, Elvis' personal physician, Dr. George Nichopolous (below), would become a figure of feverish speculation concerning Elvis' drug dependence.

"I WISH HE NEVER DIED MYSELF, SO I WOULDN'T HAVE TO HEAR ABOUT HIM EVERY SINGLE DAY."
Spike Lee, director

Elvis: What Happened?), had been asked by Colonel Parker and Vernon Presley to investigate the source of Elvis' growing drug supplies. It also came out that in 1975 Priscilla had confronted Elvis about his problem and suggested that he be secretly hospitalized. This information tied in with the fact that Elvis had entered the Baptist Memorial Hospital in Memphis many times during that year.

REPORTEDLY, MANY OF THE drugs had been supplied by Dr. Elias Ghanem, a Las Vegas physician who treated many show business people. However, the main supplier was indicated as Dr. George Constantine Nichopoulos, Elvis' personal physician in Memphis and on the road. Nichopoulos, or "Dr. Nick," came under the spotlight shortly after the disclosures about Elvis' drug dependence. Widely accused of encouraging Elvis' drug habit, Nichopoulos was eventually reprimanded and barred from practising, following an investigation by Geraldo Rivera on ABC-TV's "20/20" program and a subsequent inquest by the Tennessee Medical Board.

ELVIS' BODY WAS HARDLY cold when Colonel Parker came to a deal with Vernon to form Boxcar Enterprises, a management-merchandising company

166

The growing speculations about Elvis' drug dependence, added to the almost paranoid secrecy regarding examination of his body, did not help to ease the grief of those closest to Elvis, such as his white-haired father, Vernon (left), shown being helped out of the mausoleum after the final funeral services for his son. Meanwhile, the fans continued to line Elvis Presley Boulevard (below), asking the drivers of passing cars to switch on their headlights in respect for the dead King.

created to promote Elvis products and the Presley estate. A spin-off came in the shape of Factors Inc., a Delaware merchandizing firm designated by Parker to flood the market with "authorized" Elvis souvenirs.

BY THE FOLLOWING YEAR, Parker would be holding his first "Always Elvis" convention at the Las Vegas Hilton. He would soon adopt it as his marketing-promotion slogan and authorize its use as the name of a white wine marketed by the Italian firm of Franenac, for distribution and sale in the U.S. This particularly incensed many Elvis fans because it was well known that Elvis never drank wine.

IN THE FIRST THREE years after his death, the Elvis Presley estate made $20 million from record sales and products. Thereafter, the annual income kept rising.

IN OCTOBER 9, 1977, a book called *The Illustrated Elvis*, written by British novelist and fan W.A. Harbinson two years before Elvis' death, was number one on the U.S. bestseller lists. A whole string of other Elvis books, generated by his untimely death, was to follow, creating a minor publishing industry.

ONLY DAYS AFTER THE funeral, Vernon and Dee Presley were divorced. Dee then holed up with her three sons and writer Martin Torgoff to put together *Elvis: We Love You Tender*. The resulting work received a critical drubbing when it was published. In a later book, *The Complete Elvis*, Torgoff defended his collaboration with Dee Presley and her boys by insisting it had been a labor of love. Many subsequent books about Elvis were described in the same way by their authors, though the contents of few would support such claims. Books about Elvis' scandalous private life were warmly received by publishers; those devoted to his art had a hard time.

MOST OF THE MEMPHIS MAFIA, and even certain of Elvis' relatives, cashed in on his death either with books, by giving interviews to the media and talks at fan conventions, or by sponsoring Elvis "products" of all kinds.

SHORTLY AFTER VERNON'S DIVORCE, Ginger Alden claimed that Elvis had been planning to marry her on Christmas day of 1977. This claim was disputed by many who knew Elvis. Undeterred, Ginger's mother, Jo Alden, filed a $40,000 lawsuit against the Presley estate, claiming that Elvis had agreed to pay the mortgage on her home and provide improvements in return for letting Ginger travel with him on tour.

IN 1978, THE ACCLAIMED young film director John Carpenter directed the Dick Clark production of *Elvis*, an ABC-TV movie starring Kurt Russell as an unlikely, deeply mournful Elvis and Shelly Winters as his doting, whining mother. The movie, which painted Elvis as a totally humorless, fame-obsessed manic-depressive haunted by his dead twin, was steeped in a pervading atmosphere of

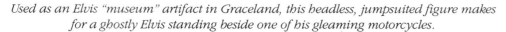
Used as an Elvis "museum" artifact in Graceland, this headless, jumpsuited figure makes for a ghostly Elvis standing beside one of his gleaming motorcycles.

gloom; nevertheless, it achieved the highest ratings in the history of ABC-TV.

THE STAR, KURT RUSSELL, had made his movie debut playing the boy who kicks Elvis in the leg in *It Happened at the World's Fair* (1962). He thrilled Elvis fans a third time by marrying Season Hubley, who portrayed Priscilla in the TV *Elvis*.

COUNTRY AND WESTERN SINGER Candy Jo Fuller claimed to be Elvis' illegitimate daughter by her mother, Terri Taylor, who insisted that she and Elvis had carnal knowledge of one another in the 1950s. They therefore also insisted that Candy's son, Michael, was Elvis' grandson. Competition came, inevitably, with *Are you Lonesome Tonight? The Untold Story of Elvis Presley's One True Love – and the Child He Never Knew* (1987) by Lucy de Barbin with Dary Matera.

SMALL WONDER THAT THROUGHOUT the 1980s thousands of people were convinced that they had either seen the real Elvis, still alive and well, or had spoken to him from beyond the grave.

BY 1990 THERE WERE hundreds of Elvis Presley imitators, some of whom were earning as much as $15,000 per week playing at Las Vegas. Countless "tribute" records were recorded, many trashy, but the significance of Elvis in the culture was given full measure in the songs of many major singer-songwriters, including Bob Dylan, Laurie Anderson, Paul Simon, Don McLean, Warren Zevon, Bruce Springsteen, Robbie Robertson, David Byrne of Talking Heads, Bono of U2, and even Led Zeppelin. At the time of writing (January 1992), the latest single by Dire Straits is entitled "Calling Elvis" and a brand-new recording artist, Marc Cohn, has had a hit with "Walking in Memphis," a song about a visit to Memphis in general and Graceland (and the ghost of Elvis) in particular. Also, Elvis has been used as an image in numerous works of serious fiction, including those by Ian McEwen and Margaret Atwood, as well as in movies, such as Jim Jarmusch's *Mystery Train* and David Lynch's *Wild at Heart*. British singer-songwriter Elvis Costello has not only written about Elvis, but stolen his name. Many contemporary artists, including Andy Warhol, have used Elvis as the inspiration for their paintings.

THE TWO-ROOM SHACK in which Elvis was born is now a State Historical Monument. It is still located on the Old Saltillo Road, though this is now named Elvis Presley Drive, in an area known as Presley Heights. The former shack was smartened up, courtesy of the East Heights Garden Club, in the style of the 1930s. It is now surrounded by the Elvis Memorial Chapel, Elvis Presley Park, including a club house, swimming pool, baseball field (Presley Field), playing areas for children, and the mandatory Elvis Presley memorabilia shops. Highway 78, running between Tupelo and Memphis, has been renamed the Elvis Aaron Presley Memorial Highway.

THE HICKORY LOG, A small cafe owned by Bonnie and Hobert Burnette, located on Elvis Presley Boulevard, has become an unofficial gathering place for Elvis fans visiting Memphis.

One of Graceland's most popular attractions is a walk through Elvis' touring plane, the Lisa Marie. *This is a Convair 880 jet complete with bedroom, conference room and lounge.*

A shockingly aged Vernon Presley attended the "Always Elvis" convention organized by Colonel Parker at Las Vegas to commemorate the first anniversary of Elvis' death. Both the convention and the bronze lifesize Elvis statue unveiled outside the Hilton showroom were reviled by journalists and fans as tasteless exploitation.

173

A BRONZE STATUE OF Elvis, sculpted by Carl Romanelli, was unveiled by Vernon and Priscilla on September 8, 1978, near the entrance to the Las Vegas Hilton showroom. The showroom was dedicated to Elvis. Many Elvis mementos, including the jumpsuit worn for his "Aloha From Hawaii" satellite show, were also put on display at the Hilton. On August 14, 1980, another large bronze statue of Elvis, sculpted by Eric Parks, was unveiled in Elvis Presley Plaza, Memphis, south of the downtown area. In London, Madam Tussaud's unveiled a waxwork Elvis that outraged many fans.

Elvis' customized Cadillac of sprayed gold, with gold trim (above) and his many awards for his contributions to music and various humanitarian causes (left) are just some of the many items now on display at Graceland.

SINCE ELVIS' PASSING, NUMEROUS radio stations worldwide have featured special "Elvis" programs on an annual basis, usually built around his birthday or the anniversary of his death. Radio KRLA in Pasadena, California, airs an hour of Elvis every night. Other, smaller stations play nothing but Elvis records. Sam Phillips' ultimate tribute to Elvis was to change the name of his Memphis radio station to WLVS.

THE FIRST FORMALLY-ACCREDITED university level course on Elvis was taught at the University of Tennessee in 1980. It was entitled *Cultural Phenomenon of Elvis Presley: The Making of a Folk Hero.*

IN 1981, A THREE-HOUR documentary film, *This is Elvis*, attempted to cover the whole span of Elvis' life with a mixture of a fake Elvis and friends and relatives,

175

dramatized scenes of his childhood and adolescence, home movies, newsreels, and documentary footage of the real Elvis at work and play. This being an "authorized" version of events, it is sometimes not believable and often annoying; finally, however, it is a riveting portrait of an American odyssey from impoverished anonymity to unprecedented fame and ultimate tragedy. The final scenes of a bloated, sweating Elvis singing "My Way" during his last performance, followed by a montage of the glorious young Elvis, have an overwhelming emotional impact.

APPOINTED EXECUTOR OF ELVIS' will in August of 1977, Vernon Presley did his best to deal with its complexities, but eventually, with his spirit broken and health visibly failing, he took Sandy Miller in as his nurse, house-mate and girlfriend. She remained with him until he died on June 26, 1979.

IN JULY OF 1981 Memphis attorney Blanchard Toole was appointed as the guardian of Lisa Marie Presley and brought suit against Colonel Tom Parker, claiming that Parker was no longer entitled to half of Elvis' earnings for life. He also claimed that the Colonel, and perhaps RCA Records, had defrauded the Presley estate of over two million dollars. The probate judge accused Parker of "violating his duty to Elvis and to the estate (by charging commissions) that were … excessive, imprudent … and beyond all reasonable bounds of industry standards."

COLONEL PARKER, NOW IN his early eighties, is living in Las Vegas and planning to make a movie that will set people straight on the record of his involvement with Elvis.

IN 1982 PRISCILLA FORMED Elvis Presley Enterprises and opened Graceland to the public. Her $500,000 investment was repaid in thirty-eight days and Graceland is now the most visited American home after the White House. Priscilla is a trustee of the Elvis Presley estate, along with family accountant Joseph Hanks and the National Bank of Commerce in Memphis. She has also been a successful model and co-starred in the two hugely successful *Naked Gun* movies.

ON FEBRUARY 1, 1993, when she turns twenty-five, Lisa Marie will inherit the Elvis Presley estate, now estimated as being worth $75 million, with an estimated $15 million being added each year.

IN 1990, "MY HAPPINESS," the first song Elvis ever recorded (on that $4 Sun acetate, possibly for his mother) was discovered and released as the lead track on an otherwise unremarkable compilation album, *The Great Performances*, thus bringing the Elvis Presley story full circle.

TO DATE, MORE THAN one billion Elvis records have been sold – enough to circle the globe twice.

IN OTHER WORDS, ELVIS continues to be heard all over the world and is still giving pleasure to millions.

YOU CAN'T KEEP A good man down.

The deification of Elvis included sightings of him, cassettes of him speaking from beyond the grave, and illustrations of Elvis as a heavenly creature (right).

Priscilla Presley (above) is now a trustee of the Elvis Presley estate. Lisa Marie (top) will inherit the estate when she turns twenty-five in February, 1993.

Bibliography

T

HERE ARE NOW LITERALLY hundreds of books about Elvis Presley, ranging in quality from the sublime to the ridiculous. Listed below are the ones considered by this author to be among the most valuable.

The memory of Elvis will not die and has spawned many minor industries, most notably in memorabilia, bootleg records, videotapes and books. While everyone seems to have their own favorite Elvis period, his whole life, from birth to death, is now relentlessly explored and exploited by academics, fans and merchandizers. In this sense, Elvis is now more popular than ever.

ELVIS AND GLADYS (Weidenfeld & Nicolson, London, 1985; MacMillan, New York, 1985) by Elaine Dundy. The definitive study of Elvis' family history, childhood, and early fame. Dundy writes with a novelist's perception and respect for her subject.

BEALE BLACK AND BLUE (Louisiana State University Press, Baton Rouge and London, 1981) by Margaret McKee and Fred Chisenhall. The book proves conclusively (contrary to Albert Goldman) that Elvis often visited Beale Street and performed there when still in his teens.

ELVIS '56: IN THE BEGINNING (Collier Books, New York, 1979) by Alfred Wertheimer. Subtitled *An Intimate Eyewitness Photo-Journal*, this follows Elvis on tour in the early days. Fabulous photos and truly evocative, affectionate text. This is a "must" for any Elvis library.

ELVIS (Simon & Schuster, New York, 1971, Abacus, London, 1974) and *Elvis: The Final Years* (St. Martin's Press, New York, 1980, W.H. Allen London, 1980), both by Jerry Hopkins. The former was the first biography on Elvis; the second is self-explanatory. Written with great wit and affection, combined the books give a panoramic view of Elvis from birth to death – though recent revelations have, understandably, rendered the first volume inaccurate in certain details.

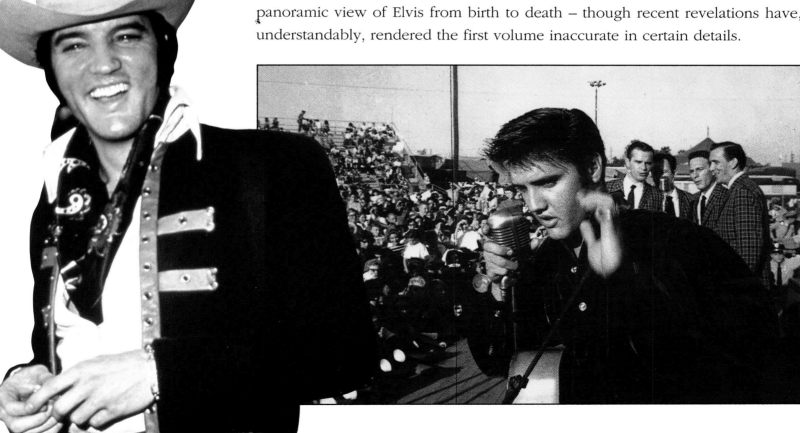

179

THE COMPLETE ELVIS (Delilah Communications, New York, 1982) edited by Martin Torgoff. A well illustrated, large-format paperback containing articles by professional writers and fans, plus an invaluable A-Z, compiled with the help of the British Elvis fan club.

ELVIS AND ME (Putnam's, New York, 1985) by Priscilla Beaulieu Presley with Sandra Harmon. Written as a bland romance with the odd bizarre twist and invented dialogue. Of value only because Priscilla was Elvis' one and only wife.

ELVIS: WHAT HAPPENED? (Ballantine, New York, 1977, William Collins, London, 1977) by Red West, Sonny West, and Dave Hebler, as told to Steve Dunleavy. The book that shocked Elvis – and his fans. Love it or loathe it, it is now part of Elvis' history.

ELVIS (McGraw-Hill, New York, 1981) by Albert Goldman. The *Mein Kampf* of Elvis biographies. Goldman despises poor southerners, rock-and-roll in general, and Elvis Presley in particular. His epic is packed with inaccuracies, suppositions, and questionable dialogue. Nevertheless, Goldman must be credited with discovering previously unknown facts about Elvis and Colonel Parker.

MYSTERY TRAIN: IMAGES OF AMERICA IN ROCK 'N' ROLL MUSIC (E.P. Dutton, New York, 1975, Omnibus Press, London, 1977) and *Dead Elvis: A Chronicle of Cultural Obsession* (Doubleday, New York, 1991) by Griel Marcus. The former contains Marcus' important essay, *Elvis: Preslaid*; the latter is all about the bizarre varieties of cultural obsession spawned by the death of Elvis. It also includes the definitive "demolition" job on Albert Goldman's notorious biography.

ELVIS (Rolling Stone Press, New York, 1992; Elm Tree Books, London, 1982) by Dave Marsh. Written by another academic and former *Rolling Stone* journalist (as is Griel Marcus, above), and designed by Bea Feitler, this is a lavish, almost perfect marriage between text and photographs.

ELVIS: AN ILLUSTRATED BIOGRAPHY (Michael Joseph, London, 1975) by W.A. Harbinson is the book that went to number one on the New York bestseller lists shortly after Elvis' death. It has been republished many times in various shapes and sizes, including *The Illustrated Elvis* (Grosset & Dunlap, New York, 1976; Perigree, New York, 1987); *The Life and Death of Elvis Presley* (Michael Joseph, London, 1977); and *The Legend of Elvis Presley* (Treasure Press, London, 1988).

ELVIS: IMAGES AND FANCIES (University Press of Mississippi, 1981) edited by Jac L. Tharpe is a collection of the more academic essays on Elvis, invaluable to the serious scholar.

THE GREAT AMERICAN POPULAR SINGERS (Gollancz, London, 1974) by Henry Pleasants. Written by a distinguished music critic. The essay on Elvis includes an analysis of his extraordinary vocal range and singing technique.

That the Elvis of the 'fifties retains his magical radiance is most evident in the superb books of Tutti Frutti Productions, Amsterdam, Holland. The most recent are Faces and Stages: An Elvis Presley Time-Frame *and* Fire in the Sun. *They are found mostly in specialist bookshops.*

Whether as humble soldier or bejeweled Sun King, Elvis is, for many, more alive in death than he was in life.

ELVIS PRESLEY: A STUDY IN MUSIC (Midas Books, Tunbridge Wells, 1979) by Robert Matthew-Walker. Another examination of the music, as well as the man. This is a good one to dip into when you're listening to Elvis records. Comment is passed on every single Elvis recording.

ALL ABOUT ELVIS (Bantam, New York, 1981) by Fred L. Worth and Steve D. Tamerius. A massive compilation of Elvis trivia and discographies.

RECORDING SESSIONS (Jee Publications, Denmark, 1975, 1977) by Ernst Jorgensen, Erik Rasmussen, and Johnny Mikkelsen. Paperback guide to every Elvis recording session, including dates, locations, musicians and matrix numbers.

ELVIS: THE ILLUSTRATED DISCOGRAPHY (Omnibus, London, 1981) by Martin Hawkins and Colin Escott, includes a good listing of bootlegs.

ELVIS: THE COMPLETE ILLUSTRATED RECORD (Eel Pie Publishing, London, 1982) is a lavish, large-format paperback that also details all the recordings, legitimate and illegitimate, with text by two rock-and-roll purists.

The formally-accredited university level course on Elvis, first taught at the University of Tennessee in 1980, was only the beginning of what is now a broad academic reappraisal of Elvis' place in modern-day culture. For this reason, the quality of research on Elvis' recording sessions improves every year and already is more comprehensive than that existing on any other singer.

183

Filmography
Feature Films

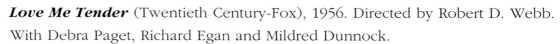

Though it is widely conceded that the promise shown by Elvis as an actor was never realized - or more accurately, was destroyed by mismanagement - even his worst movies continue to make fortunes in video formats, testifying to his enduring popularity.

Love Me Tender (Twentieth Century-Fox), 1956. Directed by Robert D. Webb. With Debra Paget, Richard Egan and Mildred Dunnock.

Loving You (Paramount), 1957. Directed by Hal Kanter. With Lizbeth Scott, Wendell Corey and Dolores Hart.

Jailhouse Rock (MGM), 1957. Directed by Richard Thorpe. With Judy Tyler, Mickey Shaughnessy and Dean Jones.

King Creole (Paramount), 1958. Directed by Michael Curtiz. With Carolyn Jones, Dolores Hart, Walter Matthau, Dean Jagger, Jan Shepard, Vic Morrow and Liliane Montevecchi.

GI Blues (Paramount), 1960. Directed by Norman Taurog. With Juliet Prowse and James Douglas.

Flaming Star (Twentieth Century-Fox), 1960. Directed by Don Siegel. With Barbara Eden, Steve Forrest, John McIntire and Dolores del Rio.

Wild in the Country (Twentieth Century-Fox), 1960. Directed by Philip Dunne. With Hope Lange, John Ireland, Tuesday Weld, Millie Perkins and Gary Lockwood.

Blue Hawaii (Paramount), 1961. Directed by Norman Taurog. With Angela Lansbury, Joan Blackman, Roland Winters and Nancy Walters.

Follow that Dream (United Artists), 1961. Directed by Gordon Douglas. With Arthur O'Connell, Joanna Moore and Anne Helm.

Kid Galahad (United Artists), 1961. Directed by Phil Karlson. With Gig Young, Lola Albright, Charles Bronson and Joan Blackman.

Girls! Girls! Girls! (Paramount), 1962. Directed by Norman Taurog. With Stella Stevens, Laurel Goodwin and Jeremy Slate.

It Happened at the World's Fair (MGM), 1962. Directed by Norman Taurog. With Joan O'Brien, Gary Lockwood and Yvonne Craig.

Fun in Acapulco (Paramount), 1963. Directed by Richard Thorpe. With Ursula Andress, Paul Lukas and Alejandro Rey.

Viva Las Vegas (MGM), 1963. Directed by George Sidney. With Ann-Margret, Cesare Danova and William Demarest.

Kissin' Cousins (MGM), 1963. Directed by Gene Nelson. With Arthur O'Connell, Glenda Farrell, Pamela Austin and Yvonne Craig.

Roustabout (Paramount), 1964. (UK title: Love in Las Vegas) Directed by John Rich. With Barbara Stanwyck, Joan Freeman and Sue Ane Langdon.

Girl Happy (MGM), 1964. Directed by Boris Sagal. With Shelley Fabares, Mary Ann Mobley, Chris Noel and Joby Baker.

Tickle Me (Allied Artists Picture Corporation), 1964. Directed by Norman Taurog. With Jocelyn Lane, Julie Adams, Jack Mullaney and Merry Anders.

185

Harum Scarum (MGM) (UK title: Harem Holiday), 1965. Directed by Gene Nelson. With Mary Ann Mobley and Fran Jeffries.

Frankie and Johnny (United Artists), 1965. Directed by Frederick de Cordova. With Donna Douglas, Harry Morgan, Nancy Kovack and Sue Ane Langdon.

Paradise, Hawaiian Style (Paramount), 1966. Directed by Michael Moore. With Suzanna Leigh, James Shigeta and Donna Butterworth.

Spinout (MGM) (UK title: California Holiday), 1966. Directed by Norman Taurog. With Shelley Fabares, Diane McBain and Deborah Walley.

Double Trouble (MGM), 1966. Directed by Norman Taurog. With Annette Day, John Williams, Yvonne Romain, the Wiere Brothers, and Chips Rafferty.

Easy Come, Easy Go (Paramount), 1966. Directed by John Rich. With Dodie Marshall, Pat Priest and Elsa Lanchester.

Clambake (United Artists), 1967. Directed by Arthur H. Nadel. With Shelley Fabares, Bill Bixby, Will Hutchins and Gary Merrill.

Speedway (MGM), 1967. Directed by Norman Taurog. With Nancy Sinatra, Bill Bixby and Gale Gordon.

Stay Away, Joe (MGM), 1967. Directed by Peter Tewksbury. With Burgess Meredith, Joan Blondell, Katy Jurado and L.Q. Jones.

Live a Little, Love a Little (MGM), 1968. Directed by Norman Taurog. With Rudy Vallee, Eddie Hodges and Michele Carey.

Charro! (National General Picture Corporation), 1968. Directed by Charles Marquis Warren. With Ina Balin, Victor French and Barbara Werle.

The Trouble with Girls [And How to Get into it] (MGM), 1968. Directed by Peter Tewksbury. With Sheree North, Marilyn Mason, Vincent Price and John Carradine.

Change of Habit (NBC-Universal), 1969. Directed by William Graham. With Mary Tyler Moore and Barbara McNair.

Documentaries

Elvis: That's the Way it is (MGM), 1970. Directed by Denis Sanders.

Elvis on Tour (MGM), 1972. Directed by Pierre Adidge and Robert Abel. Winner of the Golden Globe award for Best Documentary.

This is Elvis (Warner Bros. Inc.), 1981. Directed by Andrew Solt and Malcolm Leo. Documentary spanning Elvis' career, but with David Scott, Paul Boensch and Johnny Harra as Elvis at various ages. Lawrence Koller as Vernon, Rhonda Lyn as Priscilla, and Debbie Edge as Gladys.

THE THREE ELVIS DOCUMENTARIES and most of his feature films are available on video. Numerous other documentary videos are also available, but many are pirated and of poor quality, some do not include Elvis at all, and others are composed of recycled material disguised with new titles and covers.

APART FROM FEATURE FILMS and documentaries, the indispensable videos are:

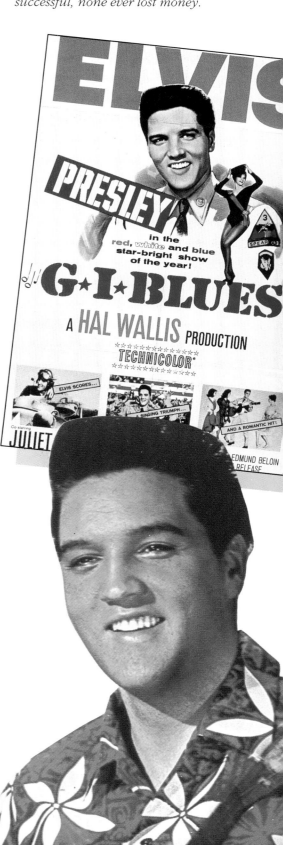

Compared to some of Elvis' movies, even GI Blues and Blue Hawaii provided good popular entertainment. While some Elvis movies were only moderately successful, none ever lost money.

King Creole (above) was possibly Elvis' finest movie, while Speedway was probably one of his worst. However, some prefer the latter to the former, which says it all about Elvis!

Elvis '68 Comeback Special. This is the historical NBC-TV Special directed by Steve Binder, but the official video release includes great material deleted from the original fifty-minute show.

Elvis Presley: One Night with You. For the above-named TV Special, Elvis held two informal, fifty-minute jamming sessions in front of a live audience, accompanied by Scotty Moore, J.D. Fontana, Charlie Hodge and Alan Fortas. Only selected extracts were used for the TV special. This is the filmed record of the first complete session. Elvis plays a mean guitar and sings some of his greatest hits. He never looked or sounded better than he does on this particular video.

Elvis: The Great Performances, *Volume One: Center Stage* and *Volume Two: The Man and his Music*. A complementary twin-set. The packaging includes illustrated booklets with exemplary text by Peter Guralnick. Elvis from start to finish, but with genuinely rare material and an intelligent selection from his onstage, TV and movie performances. Written and directed by Andrew Solt (*This is Elvis*), also Executive Producer, these two videos are proud vindication of the Elvis Presley Estate's determination to put a halt to inferior Elvis bootlegs.

ALSO AVAILABLE ON VIDEO is the fictionalized biographical movie, *Elvis* (Dick Clark Motion Pictures Inc.), 1979, directed by John Carpenter, with Kurt Russell as Elvis, Shelly Winters as Gladys, Season Hubley as Priscilla, and Pat Hingle as Col. Tom Parker.

187

Discography

A COMPLETE DISCOGRAPHY OF all Elvis Presley products would take up more space than this book can comfortably afford. Because so much of the current Elvis catalogue consists of compilations and repackages, the following is a selection of the most important albums. As singles, EPs and bootlegs are now in the province of dedicated collectors, they have not been included. Catalogue numbers differ here and in other countries, and have been changed many times for different releases, so their inclusion would be of little help to the reader.

1954-1958

THE SUN SESSIONS: That's all Right [Mama]/Blue Moon of Kentucky/I Don't Care if the Sun Don't Shine/Good Rockin' Tonight/Milkcow Blues Boogie/You're a Heartbreaker/I'm Left, You're Right, She's Gone/Baby Let's Play House/Mystery Train/I Forgot to Remember to Forget/I'll Never Let You Go [Little Darlin']/I Love You Because/Trying to Get to You/Blue Moon/Just Because

ROCK 'N' ROLL: Blue Suede Shoes/I'm Counting on You/I Got a Woman/One-Sided Love Affair/I Love You Because/Just Because/Tutti Frutti/Trying to Get to You/I'm Gonna Sit Right Down and Cry/I'll Never Let You Go/Blue Moon/Money Honey

ROCK 'N' ROLL No 2 (U.S. title: ELVIS): Rip it Up/Love Me/When my Blue Moon Turns to Gold Again/Long Tall Sally/First in Line/Paralyzed/So Glad You're Mine/Old Shep/Ready Teddy/Anyplace is Paradise/How's the World Treating You/How Do You Think I Feel

LOVING YOU: Mean Woman Blues/Teddy Bear/Loving You/Got a Lot O' Livin' to Do/Lonesome Cowboy/Hot Dog/Party/Blueberry Hill/True Love/Don't Leave Me Now/Have I Told You Lately That I Love You/I Need You So

ELVIS' CHRISTMAS ALBUM: Santa Claus is Back in Town/White Christmas/Here Comes Santa Claus/I'll Be Home for Christmas/Blue Christmas/Santa Bring my Baby Back to Me/O Little Town of Bethlehem/Silent Night/Peace in the Valley/I Believe/Take my Hand, Precious Lord/It is No Secret

KING CREOLE: King Creole/As Long as I Have You/Hard Headed Woman/Dixieland Rock/Don't Ask Me Why/Lover Doll/Young Dreams/Crawfish/Steadfast, Loyal and True/New Orleans

1960-1968

ELVIS IS BACK Make Me Know it/Fever/The Girl of my Best Friend/I Will be Home Again/Dirty Dirty Feeling/The Thrill of your Love/Soldier Boy/Such a Night/Feels so Right/The Girl Next Door/Like a Baby/Reconsider Baby

HIS HAND IN MINE: His Hand in Mine/I'm Gonna Walk Dem Golden Stairs/In my Father's House/Milky White Way/Known Only to Him/I Believe in the Man in the Sky/Joshua Fit the Battle/He Knows Just What I Need/Swing Down Sweet Chariot/Mansion over the Hilltop/If We Never Meet Again/Working on the Building

SOMETHING FOR EVERYBODY: There's Always Me/Give Me the Right/It's a Sin/Sentimental Me/Starting Today/Gently/I'm Coming Home/In your Arms/Put the Blame on Me/Judy/I Want You with Me/I Slipped, I Stumbled, I Fell

BLUE HAWAII: Blue Hawaii/Almost Always True/Aloha Oe/No More/Can't Help Falling in Love/Rock-a-Hula-Baby/Moonlight Swim/Ku-u-i-po/Ito Eats/Slicin' Sand/Hawaiian Sunset/Beach Boy Blues/Island of Love [Kauai]/Hawaiian Wedding Song

ELVIS FOR EVERYONE: Your Cheating Heart/Summer Kisses, Winter Tears/ Finders, Keepers, Losers, Weepers/In my Way/Tomorrow Night/Memphis Tennessee/For the Millionth and Last Time/Forget Me Never/Sound Advice/ Santa Lucia/Met Her Today/When it Rains it Really Pours

HOW GREAT THOU ART: How Great Thou Art/In the Garden/Somebody Bigger than You and I/Farther Along/Stand by Me/Without Him/So High/Where Could I Go but to the Lord/By and by/If the Lord Wasn't Walking by my Side/Run on/ Where No one Stands Alone/Crying in the Chapel

1968-1977

ELVIS NBC-TV SPECIAL: Trouble/Guitar Man/Lawdy Miss Clawdy/Baby What You Want Me to Do/Heartbreak Hotel/Hound Dog/All Shook Up/Can't Help Falling in Love/Jailhouse Rock/Love Me Tender/Where Could I Go but to the Lord/ Up Above my Head/Saved/Blue Christmas/One Night/Memories/Nothingville/ Big Boss Man/Guitar Man/Little Egypt/Trouble/If I Can Dream

FROM ELVIS IN MEMPHIS: Wearing that Loved on Look/Only the Strong Survive/I'll Hold You in my Heart/Long Black Limousine/It Keeps Right on a-Hurtin'/I'm Movin' on/Power of my Love/Gentle on my Mind/After Loving You/ True Love Travels on a Gravel Road/Any Day Now/In the Ghetto

FROM MEMPHIS TO VEGAS – FROM VEGAS TO MEMPHIS: Record 1: Blue Suede Shoes/Johnny B. Goode/All Shook Up/Are You Lonesome Tonight/Hound Dog/I Can't Stop Loving You/My Babe/Mystery Train/Tiger Man/Words/In the Ghetto/Suspicious Minds/Can't Help Falling in Love; Record 2: Inherit the Wind/ This is the Story/Stranger in my Own Home Town/A Little Bit of Green/And the Grass Won't Pay No Mind/Do You Know Who I Am/From a Jack to a Queen/The Fair's Moving on/You'll Think of Me/Without Love

Perhaps the most valuable aspect of the growing flood of Elvis product is the television, video and home-movie footage that is coming to light. This makes it a fascinating field for the collector, who can either watch Elvis in the cinema documentaries, or catch fascinating glimpses of him in silent movies shot years ago by family and friends. The contrasts are startling.

Yes, indeed, Elvis lives!

ON STAGE: See See Rider/Release Me/Sweet Caroline/Runaway/The Wonder of You/Polk Salad Annie/Yesterday/Proud Mary/Walk a Mile in my Shoes

THAT'S THE WAY IT IS: I Just Can't Help Believin'/Twenty Days and Twenty Nights/How the Web Was Woven/Patch it Up/Mary in the Morning/You Don't Have to Say You Love Me/You've Lost that Loving Feeling/I've Lost You/Just Pretend/Strange in the Crowd/The Next Step is Love/Bridge Over Troubled Water

ELVIS COUNTRY: Snowbird/Tomorrow Never Comes/Little Cabin on the Hill/Whole Lotta Shakin' Goin' On/Funny How Time Slips Away/I Really Don't Want to Know/There Goes my Everything/It's Your Baby, You Rock it/The Fool/Faded Love/Washed my Hands in Muddy Water/Make the World Go Away

ALOHA FROM HAWAII VIA SATELLITE: See See Rider/Burning Love/Something/You Gave Me a Mountain/Steamroller Blues/My Way/Love Me/Johnny B. Goode/It's Over/Blue Suede Shoes/I'm So Lonesome I Could Cry/I Can't Stop Loving You/Hound Dog/What Now my Love/Fever/Welcome to my World/Suspicious Minds/I'll Remember You/Long Tall Sally/Whole Lotta Shakin' Goin' On/American Trilogy/A Big Hunk O' Love/Can't Help Falling in Love

MOODY BLUE: Unchained Melody/If You Love Me (Let Me Know)/Little Darlin'/He'll Have to Go/Let Me be There/Way Down/Pledging my Love/Moody Blue/She Thinks I Still Care/It's Easy for You

ALSO INDISPENSABLE ARE *Elvis' Golden Records* volumes 1 to 4, which include the classic Elvis singles not listed above, as well as the songs from *Love Me Tender, Jailhouse Rock,* and *Viva Las Vegas.*

THE LEGENDARY "MILLION DOLLAR QUARTET" turns out to be a trio consisting of Elvis, Jerry Lee Lewis and Carl Perkins. The recordings they made together are now available on an album entitled *The Million Dollar Quartet.* In fact, although Johnny Cash is shown on the cover, he does not sing on the record.

MOST OF THE BETTER SINGLES from the poor film soundtracks can be found on compilation albums or in box sets which are now too numerous to list. However, as these include such classics as "Return to Sender," "Bossa Nova Baby," "Tomorrow is a Long Time," "Suspicious Minds," "Separate Ways," "Burning Love," "Promised Land," "Loving Arms," and the often superb, so-called "bonus" tracks, a thorough study of the ever-changing Elvis catalogue is recommended.

Elvis Presley

JANUARY 8, 1935 ~ AUGUST 16, 1977

COMMUNIT FAIR NIG